W9-CRK-468

Daily
GRADE 2

Reading
Comprehension

Writing: Karen Cardella
Content Editing: Marilyn Evans
James Spears
Copy Editing: Carrie Gwynne
Art Direction: Cheryl Puckett
Cover Design: Cheryl Puckett
Design/Production: Carolina Caird
Arynne Elfenbein
Yuki Meyer
Marcia Smith

EMC 3452

Evan-Moor®
EDUCATIONAL PUBLISHERS
Helping Children Learn since 1979

Visit
teaching-standards.com
to view a correlation
of this book.
This is a free service.

***Correlated to State and
Common Core State Standards***

**Congratulations on your purchase of some of the
finest teaching materials in the world.**

*Photocopying the pages in this book
is permitted for <u>single-classroom use only</u>.
Making photocopies for additional classes
or schools is prohibited.*

Contents

Daily Reading Comprehension • EMC 3452 • © Evan-Moor Corp.

How to Use *Daily Reading Comprehension*

Daily Reading Comprehension provides a unique integration of instruction and practice in both comprehension strategies and comprehension skills.

Strategies—such as visualizing or asking questions—are general, meta-cognitive techniques that a reader uses to better understand and engage with the text. **Skills**—such as finding a main idea or identifying a sequence of events—focus on particular text elements that aid comprehension. See page 6 for a complete list of strategies and skills covered in *Daily Reading Comprehension*.

The first six weeks of *Daily Reading Comprehension* introduce students to comprehension strategies they will apply throughout the year. Weeks 7–30 focus on specific skill instruction and practice. All 30 weeks follow the same five-day format, making the teaching and learning process simpler. Follow these steps to conduct the weekly lessons and activities:

STEP 1 The weekly teacher page lists the strategy or skills that students will focus on during that week and provides a brief definition of the strategy or the skills. Read the definition(s) aloud to students each day before they complete the activities, or prompt students to define the skill(s) themselves. You may also wish to reproduce the comprehension strategy and skill definitions on page 8 as a poster for your classroom.

STEP 2 The teacher page provides an instructional path for conducting each day's lesson and activities. Use the tips and suggestions in each day's lesson to present the skills and introduce the passage.

STEP 3 Each student page begins with directions for reading the passage. These directions also serve as a way to establish a purpose for reading. Help students see the connection between setting a purpose for reading and improving comprehension.

STEP 4 Because much of reading comprehension stems from a reader's background knowledge about a subject, take a moment to discuss the topic with students before they read a passage. Introduce unfamiliar phrases or concepts, and encourage students to ask questions about the topic.

STEP 5 After students have read a passage, two comprehension activities give students an opportunity to practice the strategies and skills. In weeks 1–6, the first activity is an open-ended writing or partner activity that encourages students to reflect on the reading process, applying the weekly strategy. The second activity provides four multiple-choice items that practice the week's skills in a test-taking format.

In weeks 7–30, students complete the multiple-choice skill activity before practicing the strategy activity. The teacher page for these weeks offers suggestions for teaching the skills and gives tips for reminding students of the strategy(ies). Throughout the week, use the Student Record Sheet on page 9 to track student progress and to note which skills or strategies a student may need additional practice with.

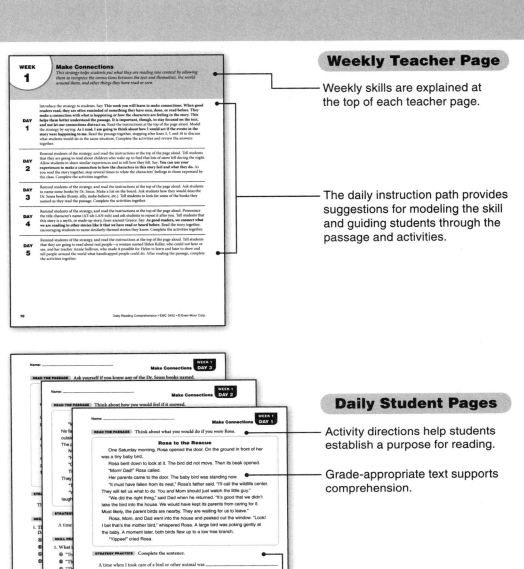

Weekly Teacher Page

Weekly skills are explained at the top of each teacher page.

The daily instruction path provides suggestions for modeling the skill and guiding students through the passage and activities.

Daily Student Pages

Activity directions help students establish a purpose for reading.

Grade-appropriate text supports comprehension.

Each passage is followed by four multiple-choice items, practicing specific comprehension skills, as well as an open-ended strategy-based activity. In weeks 1–6, the strategy activity precedes the skill activity.

Student Record Sheet

The record sheet allows you to record students' progress and identify areas in which individuals need improvement.

Comprehension Strategies and Skills

In *Daily Reading Comprehension*, students learn and practice the following commonly tested comprehension strategies and skills, all proven to increase students' abilities to read and understand a wide range of text types. You may also wish to post or distribute copies of page 8, which provides a student-friendly list of skills and helpful questions that students can ask themselves as they read.

Strategies

Make Connections
Students make connections to the text to aid their comprehension. Connections can be made to personal experiences or to things the students have seen or read.

Visualization
Students make mental images of what they are reading. They learn to look for vivid language, including concrete nouns, active verbs, and strong adjectives.

Organization
Students learn to find the organizational pattern of a text. This allows them to anticipate what they are reading and helps them focus on the author's central message or important ideas.

Determine Important Information
Students learn to categorize information based on whether or not it supports an author's central message or is important for a specific purpose.

Ask Questions
Students learn to ask questions before reading to set a purpose for reading, during reading to identify when their comprehension breaks down, or after reading as a way to check their understanding of a passage.

Monitor Comprehension
Students learn to pay attention to their own reading process and notice when they are losing focus or when comprehension is breaking down. They then can employ another strategy to help them overcome their difficulty.

Skills

Main Idea and Details
Students identify what a passage is mostly about and find important details that support the main idea.

Sequence
Students look for the order in which things happen or identify the steps in a process.

Cause and Effect
Students identify what happens (effect) and why it happens (cause).

Fact and Opinion
Students determine which statements can be proved true (fact) and which statements tell what someone thinks or believes (opinion).

Compare and Contrast
Students note how two or more people or things are alike and different.

Make Inferences
Students use their background knowledge and clues from the text to infer information.

Prediction
Students use their background knowledge and clues from the text to figure out what will happen next.

Character and Setting
Students identify who or what a story is about and where and when the story takes place.

Fantasy and Reality
Students determine whether something in a story could or could not happen in real life.

Author's Purpose
Students determine why an author wrote a passage and whether the purpose is: to entertain, to inform, to persuade, or to teach.

Nonfiction Text Features
Students study features that are not part of the main body of text, including subheadings, captions, entry words, and titles.

Visual Information
Students study pictures, charts, graphs, and other forms of visual information.

 Daily Reading Comprehension • EMC 3452 • © Evan-Moor Corp.

Scope and Sequence

	Week 30	Week 29	Week 28	Week 27	Week 26	Week 25	Week 24	Week 23	Week 22	Week 21	Week 20	Week 19	Week 18	Week 17	Week 16	Week 15	Week 14	Week 13	Week 12	Week 11	Week 10	Week 9	Week 8	Week 7	Week 6	Week 5	Week 4	Week 3	Week 2	Week 1
Comprehension Strategies																														
Make Connections		•	•					•	•					•	•					•	•									•
Visualization			•		•			•		•					•		•				•		•						•	
Organization	•				•		•			•	•						•		•				•					•		
Determine Important Information	•					•	•					•	•					•	•					•		•	•			
Ask Questions		•		•				•		•				•		•				•		•			•					
Monitor Comprehension				•		•				•		•			•		•					•		•	•					
Comprehension Skills																														
Main Idea and Details						•						•						•						•					•	
Sequence						•						•						•						•			•	•		
Cause and Effect							•				•						•						•				•	•		
Fact and Opinion							•				•						•						•				•			
Compare and Contrast				•						•					•							•			•			•		
Make Inferences				•						•					•							•								•
Prediction		•						•						•						•										
Character and Setting			•						•						•						•									•
Fantasy and Reality			•						•						•						•					•				
Author's Purpose		•						•						•						•						•				
Nonfiction Text Features	•						•						•						•								•			
Visual Information	•						•						•						•								•			

How to Be a Good Reader

Ask yourself these questions to help you understand what you read:

Main Idea and Details
What is the story mostly about?
What tells me more about the main idea?

Sequence
What happens first, next, and last?
What are the steps to do something?

Cause and Effect
What happens? (the effect)
Why did it happen? (the cause)

Fact and Opinion
Can this be proved true?
Is it what someone thinks or believes?

Compare and Contrast
How are these people or things the same?
How are these people or things different?

Make Inferences
What clues does the story give?
What do I know already that will help?

Prediction
What clues does the story give?
What do I know already that will help?
What will happen next?

Character and Setting
Who or what is the story about?
Where and when does the story take place?

Fantasy and Reality
Is it make-believe?
Could it happen in real life?

Author's Purpose
Does the story entertain, inform, try
to persuade me, or teach me how to do
something?

Nonfiction Text Features
What kind of text am I reading?
What does it tell me?

Visual Information
Is there a picture, chart, or graph?
What does it tell me?

Student Record Sheet

Student: _____

Number of Questions Answered Correctly

	Day 1	Day 2	Day 3	Day 4	Day 5	Notes:
Week 1						
Week 2						
Week 3						
Week 4						
Week 5						
Week 6						
Week 7						
Week 8						
Week 9						
Week 10						
Week 11						
Week 12						
Week 13						
Week 14						
Week 15						
Week 16						
Week 17						
Week 18						
Week 19						
Week 20						
Week 21						
Week 22						
Week 23						
Week 24						
Week 25						
Week 26						
Week 27						
Week 28						
Week 29						
Week 30						

Make Connections

This strategy helps students put what they are reading into context by allowing them to recognize the connections between the text and themselves, the world around them, and other things they have read or seen.

DAY 1

Introduce the strategy to students. Say: **This week you will learn to make connections. When good readers read, they are often reminded of something they have seen, done, or read before. They make a connection with what is happening or how the characters are feeling in the story. This helps them better understand the passage. It is important, though, to stay focused on the text, and not let our connections distract us.** Read the instructions at the top of the page aloud. Model the strategy by saying: **As I read, I am going to think about how I would act if the events in the story were happening to me.** Read the passage together, stopping after lines 3, 7, and 10 to discuss what students would do in the same situation. Complete the activities and review the answers together.

DAY 2

Remind students of the strategy, and read the instructions at the top of the page aloud. Tell students that they are going to read about children who wake up to find that lots of snow fell during the night. Allow students to share similar experiences and to tell how they felt. Say: **You can use your experiences to make a connection to how the characters in this story feel and what they do.** As you read the story together, stop several times to relate the characters' feelings to those expressed by the class. Complete the activities together.

DAY 3

Remind students of the strategy, and read the instructions at the top of the page aloud. Ask students to name some books by Dr. Seuss. Make a list on the board. Ask students how they would describe Dr. Seuss books (funny, silly, make-believe, etc.). Tell students to look for some of the books they named as they read the passage. Complete the activities together.

DAY 4

Remind students of the strategy, and read the instructions at the top of the page aloud. Pronounce the title character's name (AT-uh-LAN-tuh) and ask students to repeat it after you. Tell students that this story is a myth, or made-up story, from ancient Greece. Say: **As good readers, we connect what we are reading to other stories like it that we have read or heard before.** Read the story together, encouraging students to name similarly-themed stories they know. Complete the activities together.

DAY 5

Remind students of the strategy, and read the instructions at the top of the page aloud. Tell students that they are going to read about real people—a woman named Helen Keller, who could not hear or see, and her teacher Annie Sullivan, who made it possible for Helen to learn and later to show and tell people around the world what handicapped people could do. After reading the passage, complete the activities together.

Daily Reading Comprehension • EMC 3452 • © Evan-Moor Corp.

READ THE PASSAGE   Think about what you would do if you were Rosa.

Rosa to the Rescue

One Saturday morning, Rosa opened the door. On the ground in front of her was a tiny baby bird.

Rosa bent down to look at it. The bird did not move. Then its beak opened.

"Mom! Dad!" Rosa called.

Her parents came to the door. The baby bird was standing now.

"It must have fallen from its nest," Rosa's father said. "I'll call the wildlife center. They will tell us what to do. You and Mom should just watch the little guy."

"We did the right thing," said Dad when he returned. "It's good that we didn't take the bird into the house. We would have kept its parents from caring for it. Most likely, the parent birds are nearby. They are waiting for us to leave."

Rosa, Mom, and Dad went into the house and peeked out the window. "Look! I bet that's the mother bird," whispered Rosa. A large bird was poking gently at the baby. A moment later, both birds flew up to a low tree branch.

"Yippee!" cried Rosa.

STRATEGY PRACTICE   Complete the sentence.

A time when I took care of a bird or other animal was _____.

SKILL PRACTICE   Read the question. Fill in the bubble next to the correct answer.

1. **Who is the passage about?**
   Ⓐ a family with a pet bird
   Ⓑ a family who cares about animals
   Ⓒ a father who makes a phone call
   Ⓓ a mother who looks out the window

2. **How does Rosa know the bird is alive?**
   Ⓐ It opens its eyes.
   Ⓑ It moves its head.
   Ⓒ It moves its wing.
   Ⓓ It opens its mouth.

3. **At the end of the passage, Rosa is _____.**
   Ⓐ sad
   Ⓑ quiet
   Ⓒ worried
   Ⓓ happy

4. **Where does the passage take place?**
   Ⓐ in a park
   Ⓑ in an office
   Ⓒ at Rosa's home
   Ⓓ at Rosa's school

X 11 minutes

READ THE PASSAGE Think about how you would feel if it snowed.

"Wake up, everyone! It snowed last night," Niko called. A smile spread across his face. Niko opened the front door. Icy air rushed into the warm room. The world outside was white and soft. The car in the driveway looked like a great big pillow. The pine trees were wearing big white snow hats. Everything sparkled.

Niko was putting on his jacket and boots when his brother ran in.

"Hooray for snow!" he yelled. "Where are my gloves?"

"Come back soon for breakfast," the boys' mother said.

There were pancakes on the table when the boys came back into the house. They dropped their jackets by the door and sat down at the table.

"Thanks, Mom!" Niko said. "We found a new place to sled."

"We are going to make a snowman!" Niko's brother said. The boys' mother laughed and said, "There's nothing like snow."

STRATEGY PRACTICE Complete the sentence.

A time when I felt excited like Niko was _____.

SKILL PRACTICE Read the question. Fill in the bubble next to the correct answer.

1. What is the best title for the passage?
   Ⓐ "Trees with Hats"
   Ⓑ "The Big Breakfast"
   Ⓒ "The Lost Gloves"
   Ⓓ "Hooray for Snow!"

2. Which one is true about Niko?
   Ⓐ He is older than his brother.
   Ⓑ He wants a new sled.
   Ⓒ He likes snow.
   Ⓓ He fights with his brother.

3. Where does the passage take place?
   Ⓐ at Niko's school
   Ⓑ where Niko lives
   Ⓒ at Niko's friend's house
   Ⓓ where Niko plays soccer

4. Which of these is make-believe?
   Ⓐ trees wearing hats
   Ⓑ boys wearing boots
   Ⓒ mothers making pancakes
   Ⓓ children making snowmen

READ THE PASSAGE   Ask yourself if you know any of the Dr. Seuss books named.

Dr. Seuss

"Big A, little a, what begins with A? Aunt Annie's alligator. A…a…A" Have you ever seen these lines? They are from a book called *Dr. Seuss's ABC*.

Who was Dr. Seuss? His real name was Theodor Seuss Geisel (GUY-zul). When Theodor went to college, he wrote for a magazine. He wrote funny things. His friends thought he was funny.

A few years later, he began to write books for children. He was very good at art. He drew funny pictures for his books. One book is *The Cat in the Hat*. Another one is *Hop on Pop*. Dr. Seuss's books are different from other books.

Books by Dr. Seuss are silly. They are fun to read. Some of them show make-believe animals like the *zizzer zazzer zuzz*. Young children laugh when their parents and teachers read these books to them. Older children enjoy reading them alone.

What is your favorite Dr. Seuss book?

STRATEGY PRACTICE   Complete the sentence.

The silliest book I know is _____.

SKILL PRACTICE   Read the question. Fill in the bubble next to the correct answer.

1. The passage tells about Dr. Seuss's _____.
   Ⓐ children
   Ⓑ house
   Ⓒ parents
   Ⓓ writing

2. Which of these is <u>not</u> real?
   Ⓐ Dr. Seuss's other name
   Ⓑ teachers who read books
   Ⓒ some of Dr. Seuss's animals
   Ⓓ a man who drew funny pictures

3. Dr. Seuss was a writer and _____.
   Ⓐ teacher
   Ⓑ artist
   Ⓒ reader
   Ⓓ parent

4. Which one is most like a Dr. Seuss title?
   Ⓐ "All About the Sun"
   Ⓑ "The Roly-Poly Bazoly"
   Ⓒ "How to Build a Treehouse"
   Ⓓ "My Trip to Texas"

READ THE PASSAGE   Think about how the passage is like other stories you know.

Atalanta

Long ago and far away, there lived a princess named Atalanta. She was very beautiful. She was very strong, too.

Atalanta loved to run. She could run fast. She could run faster than the men!

When men asked Atalanta to marry them, she said no. She liked to be free. She liked to hunt and spend time in the woods.

One day, Atalanta said that she would marry any man who could run faster than her. When the big race began, Atalanta took off. She flew like an arrow. She was winning the race.

One of the men in the race had a plan. He carried three apples made of gold. During the race, he threw the apples in Atalanta's path.

Three times during the race, Atalanta stopped. She stopped to pick up a golden apple. The clever man ran past her. He won the race and became Atalanta's husband.

STRATEGY PRACTICE   Complete the sentence.

Another story about a clever character winning a race is _____.

SKILL PRACTICE   Read the question. Fill in the bubble next to the correct answer.

1. Who is the passage about?
Ⓐ a husband
Ⓑ a strong man
Ⓒ a fast runner
Ⓓ a man who hunts

2. Atalanta's husband is very _____.
Ⓐ angry
Ⓑ clever
Ⓒ funny
Ⓓ sad

3. When does the passage take place?
Ⓐ long ago
Ⓑ last week
Ⓒ yesterday
Ⓓ one year ago

4. Atalanta loses the race because _____.
Ⓐ she has to run in the woods
Ⓑ the men shoot fast arrows
Ⓒ she wants the golden apples
Ⓓ strong hunters stop her

READ THE PASSAGE Think about what it would be like if you could not see or hear.

Annie Sullivan had a hard life. She grew up alone and very poor. Annie had trouble with her eyes, too. She could not see well.

One day after Annie grew up, a family called her. They needed help with their daughter. Their little girl's name was Helen Keller. Helen needed a teacher.

Helen could not see. She could not hear either. She felt scared and alone. Annie wanted to help Helen. She wanted to be able to talk to her.

Annie tried to teach Helen sign language, a way to make words with your hands. But Helen did not understand what Annie tried to teach her.

One day by the outside water pump, Annie had an idea. She held one of Helen's hands in the water. Then Annie traced W-A-T-E-R on Helen's other hand again and again and again.

At last, Helen understood. She learned that what she was feeling had a name. Helen was on her way to a lifetime of learning.

STRATEGY PRACTICE Complete the sentence.

A time when it was hard to learn something new was _____.

SKILL PRACTICE Read the question. Fill in the bubble next to the correct answer.

1. **What is the best title for the passage?**
   - Ⓐ "How to Talk with Your Hands"
   - Ⓑ "Writing on Your Hand"
   - Ⓒ "A Good Teacher"
   - Ⓓ "How Water Feels"

2. **Where does Helen learn her first word?**
   - Ⓐ near a river
   - Ⓑ in a kitchen
   - Ⓒ in a bathtub
   - Ⓓ by a water pump

3. **How does Helen feel before Annie comes?**
   - Ⓐ alone
   - Ⓑ funny
   - Ⓒ happy
   - Ⓓ angry

4. **Using hand signs helps people _____.**
   - Ⓐ see faces
   - Ⓑ share ideas
   - Ⓒ hear sounds
   - Ⓓ smell foods

Visualization

Visualization allows readers to form mental images from the text. By visualizing, good readers turn the main ideas or events in a passage into concrete pictures in their minds. Good readers use sensory words from the text to help them visualize and adjust their mental images as they read.

DAY 1

Explain to students that this week's strategy is called *Visualization*. Say: **When good readers read or hear a story, they make pictures in their minds. They imagine what the characters and places look like. They visualize what is happening. Sometimes you can visualize things so clearly, it's almost like a movie is playing in your mind.** Read the instructions at the top of the page aloud. Inform students that they will be looking for descriptive words (adjectives) and action words (verbs). As you read the passage together, stop after each paragraph and discuss which words and phrases helped students to visualize what dolphins look like or how they act (smiling, smooth bodies, blow bubble rings, etc.). Complete the activities together.

DAY 2

Remind students of the strategy, and read the instructions at the top of the page aloud. Tell students they are going to read a true story about some unusual friends. Read the passage together. Stop after the second paragraph to model the strategy: **I visualized a huge gray elephant eating a pile of hay. A little dog was standing next to her eating dog food from a bowl.** Finish reading the story. Allow students time to share with a partner something they visualized. Then complete the second activity together.

DAY 3

Remind students of the strategy, and read the title of the passage aloud. Ask students to describe the pictures that come into their minds when they hear the title. Then tell students they are going to read about two kinds of unusual fish. Read aloud the instructions at the top of the page to set a purpose for reading. Read the passage and complete the activities together.

DAY 4

Remind students of the strategy, and read the instructions at the top of the page aloud. Ask: **Who has seen pictures of a forest fire? Do you think forest fires are good or bad?** Read the first paragraph together. Model the strategy: **When I read this paragraph, I saw towering flames destroying trees and houses.** Finish the passage and allow time for students to complete the first activity. Invite volunteers to share their responses, and then complete the second activity as a group.

DAY 5

Remind students of the strategy, and read the instructions at the top of the page aloud. Tell students to notice words and phrases that help them make vivid mental pictures. Read the passage, and allow time for students to complete the first activity. Then complete the second activity together.

Look for words that help you picture dolphins.

Dolphins

When a dolphin lifts its face from the water, it seems to be smiling at us. Dolphins look happy when they jump out of the water. They look very beautiful, too. Their smooth bodies shine in the sun.

Dolphins are playful. They play with people. They play with each other. They can blow bubble rings. Then they push the rings with their noses!

Some dolphins live in water parks. They learn how to do many tricks. They can jump through hoops. They can carry big balls on the tips of their noses. They can move on top of the water using their strong tails. People smile and clap.

Dolphins have helped us, too. They have pushed swimmers to shore or kept them safe from sharks. They have warned ships of danger.

We should help dolphins, too. We should try not to hurt dolphins with our boats. We should keep their ocean home clean.

STRATEGY PRACTICE Underline two sentences in the passage that help you to picture dolphins in your mind.

SKILL PRACTICE Read the question. Fill in the bubble next to the correct answer.

1. What is the passage about?
   Ⓐ what dolphins do
   Ⓑ when dolphins eat
   Ⓒ where dolphins go
   Ⓓ why dolphins jump

2. Which one tells that dolphins help people?
   Ⓐ They look beautiful.
   Ⓑ They save swimmers.
   Ⓒ They walk on their tails.
   Ⓓ They play with each other.

3. Because dolphins do tricks, _____.
   Ⓐ they look beautiful
   Ⓑ they help swimmers
   Ⓒ they look like they are smiling
   Ⓓ people like to watch them

4. Dolphins and children both like to _____.
   Ⓐ clap
   Ⓑ laugh
   Ⓒ play
   Ⓓ read

READ THE PASSAGE   Picture the animal friends in your mind.

There is a place in Tennessee where old elephants go to live. Each elephant has a best friend there. Most of these friends are other elephants. But an elephant named Tarra chose a dog for her best friend!

Tarra and her dog friend, Bella, go everywhere together. The two friends eat together. They sleep together, too.

One day, Bella hurt her back. She needed to rest. She rested inside the office of the people who care for the elephants. Bella rested for three weeks. She rested until her back was better.

While Bella rested, Tarra stood by a gate outside the office. She stood and stood. The nice people carried Bella out to see Tarra. Bella's tail wagged. The two friends visited every day until Bella could walk again.

Tarra and Bella are together again. To show her love, the elephant pets Bella's tummy with her great big foot!

STRATEGY PRACTICE   Tell a partner about something you pictured in your mind when you read the passage.

SKILL PRACTICE   Read the question. Fill in the bubble next to the correct answer.

1. **What is the best title for the passage?**
   Ⓐ "Big Feet"
   Ⓑ "Sick Dogs"
   Ⓒ "Great Friends"
   Ⓓ "Animal Homes"

2. **Tarra and Bella are both _____.**
   Ⓐ big
   Ⓑ small
   Ⓒ people
   Ⓓ animals

3. **Why does Bella rest in the office?**
   Ⓐ Her back is hurt.
   Ⓑ She likes the people.
   Ⓒ She is mad at Tarra.
   Ⓓ Her friend went away.

4. **How does Tarra pet Bella?**
   Ⓐ with her trunk
   Ⓑ with her foot
   Ⓒ with her tail
   Ⓓ with her ear

READ THE PASSAGE Look for words that help you picture the fish.

Fish with Lights

Deep in the ocean, it is very dark. Not much sunlight can go that far down. The fish in this water make their own light. The lights are part of their bodies.

One kind of fish that makes light is the lanternfish. They are thin and small. Some are as short as a finger. The larger ones are as long as your arm.

Some lanternfish are blue, green, or silver. The ones in the deepest water are brown or black. A yellow, green, or blue light shines from along their sides.

Another fish that makes its own light is the anglerfish. The anglerfish is round like a ball. It is brown, gray, or black. Its mouth can open very wide, and its teeth are long and sharp.

The light on the anglerfish is blue-green. It grows out of its forehead and waves back and forth. The fish uses this light to get its food. Smaller fish swim to the light. Snap!

Fish with lights are one of the many wonders of our world.

STRATEGY PRACTICE Circle words in the passage that helped you picture the anglerfish.

SKILL PRACTICE Read the question. Fill in the bubble next to the correct answer.

1. **What is the passage about?**
   - Ⓐ fish as pets
   - Ⓑ the deep ocean
   - Ⓒ fish with sharp teeth
   - Ⓓ fish that can shine

2. **When the anglerfish waves its light, _____.**
   - Ⓐ it makes pretty pictures
   - Ⓑ it can see in the dark
   - Ⓒ its food swims to it
   - Ⓓ its mouth opens wide

3. **Fish with lights live in _____.**
   - Ⓐ the deep sea
   - Ⓑ big rivers
   - Ⓒ the bright sun
   - Ⓓ dark caves

4. **How is the anglerfish different from the lanternfish?**
   - Ⓐ It is thin and small.
   - Ⓑ Its light grows out of its head.
   - Ⓒ It has a row of lights on its side.
   - Ⓓ Its light can be yellow.

READ THE PASSAGE   Picture the things forest fires do.

Fire in a forest can do much harm. Forest fires burn many trees. They burn animals' homes. Some even burn people's houses.

Fires can be terrible, but they do some good things, too. Fires clear the forest floor. They get rid of old, dry branches. This helps keep more fires from starting.

Fires make new holes in trees where birds can nest. They also make more room for new trees to grow.

Some pine cones need fire. They do not let go of their seeds without it. In forest fires, the cones drop seeds that become new baby trees. This makes the forest new.

A forest fire can be both bad and good.

STRATEGY PRACTICE   Complete the sentence.

When I read this passage, I pictured _____.

SKILL PRACTICE   Read the question. Fill in the bubble next to the correct answer.

1. **What is the best title for the passage?**
   Ⓐ "Pine Cones That Need Fire"
   Ⓑ "Fires That Burn Houses"
   Ⓒ "Good Things About Forest Fires"
   Ⓓ "Firefighters Work Hard"

2. **Fires are bad when they _____.**
   Ⓐ burn homes
   Ⓑ clear the forest floor
   Ⓒ make spots for nests
   Ⓓ make room for trees

3. **When the forest floor is clear, _____.**
   Ⓐ seeds fall out of pine cones
   Ⓑ new trees have room to grow
   Ⓒ animals get rid of dry branches
   Ⓓ birds build nests

4. **Fire helps some pine trees by _____.**
   Ⓐ getting rid of old branches
   Ⓑ chasing away birds
   Ⓒ burning their needles
   Ⓓ spreading their seeds

READ THE PASSAGE   Picture how the insects hide.

Tricky Insects

See that leaf moving in the wind? Look again. It is an insect. It just looks like a leaf! Hungry birds do not know it is a bug. They do not try to eat it.

Some butterflies look like dried leaves. They rest with their wings together to match the real leaves around them. The colorful parts of their wings are hidden until they fly away.

Another bug that wears a costume is the stick insect. It looks like its name—a stick! This insect hides in the leaves and twigs of a tree. It can turn green or brown to match the colors around it. Some stick insects are tiny. Others are a foot long.

Insects are very clever. Maybe the next time you take a walk, you will see one pretending to be something else.

STRATEGY PRACTICE   Draw to show.

This is what I think a stick insect looks like:

SKILL PRACTICE   Read the question. Fill in the bubble next to the correct answer.

1. Another good title for the passage would be _____.

    Ⓐ "Matching Colors"

    Ⓑ "Hungry Birds"

    Ⓒ "Insects and Plants"

    Ⓓ "Great Pretenders"

2. Birds do not eat leaf insects because they _____.

    Ⓐ cannot see them

    Ⓑ cannot catch them

    Ⓒ do not know they are bugs

    Ⓓ do not think they taste good

3. Some butterflies look like dried leaves so that they can _____.

    Ⓐ catch bugs

    Ⓑ rest

    Ⓒ fly away

    Ⓓ close their wings

4. One way stick insects are different from real sticks is that they _____.

    Ⓐ have legs

    Ⓑ trick birds

    Ⓒ are up in trees

    Ⓓ look like wood

Organization

By looking at how a passage or selection is organized, students can better understand the author's intent, as well as predict what information is likely to appear in the future. Common methods of organization include sequential, chronological, cause and effect, compare and contrast, and main idea.

DAY 1

Explain to students that this week's strategy is called *Organization*. Say: **When writers write, they put their ideas in a special order. This is called *organization*. Some writers tell lots of things about one topic. Some writers tell how things are alike or different. Good readers figure out how a passage is organized so that they can make sense of what they read.** Read the instructions at the top of the page aloud. Say: **The writer organized this passage so that one kind of thing was told about a picnic in each paragraph.** Read the passage together, stopping after paragraphs 2 and 4 to notice the kinds of things (main idea) talked about (comfort/nonfood items; entertainment items). Complete the activities together. When discussing the strategy practice activity, help students to recognize that paragraph 3 tells about foods that people might take for a picnic. Review the fact that the passage is organized to tell about one type of picnic supply in each paragraph.

DAY 2

Remind students of the strategy, and read the instructions at the top of the page aloud. Say: **This passage is organized to compare two kinds of cars—gasoline cars and electric cars.** Read the first paragraph together. Say: **The paragraph told us about how gas cars are both good and bad. What do you think we will read about next?** (how electric cars are both good and bad) Read the rest of the passage and complete the activities together.

DAY 3

Remind students of the strategy, and read the instructions at the top of the page aloud. Say: **Another way to organize a passage is by sequence, or to tell what happens in order from first to last. As we read this passage about how seeds grow, pay attention to the order in which things happen.** Read the passage and complete the activities together.

DAY 4

Remind students of the strategy, and read the instructions at the top of the page aloud. Say: **As we read, notice how each paragraph tells about a different stage of a butterfly's life. Organizing the passage in this way makes it easier for the reader to remember the important ideas.** Read the passage and complete the activities together.

DAY 5

Remind students of the strategy and say: **This is a fiction story. Writers can organize fiction stories in many ways.** Read the instructions at the top of the page aloud. Then say: **As we read the passage, notice whether events are told in the order they happened.** Read the passage and complete the activities together. Summarize the strategy practice activity for students. Then say: **The writer of this passage organized it in sequence, or in the order events happened.**

READ THE PASSAGE
Think about the kinds of things mentioned in each paragraph.

Packing for a Picnic

It's a sunny Saturday. Let's take a picnic to the park. What should we pack?

We'll need some things besides food. A blanket to sit on would be good. Napkins will keep our clothes and fingers clean. It would be smart to bring a sweater or jacket along in case a cool breeze blows.

Now it's time to pack the food. Sandwiches are good for picnics. They are easy to hold. You can pack them in little bags. Fruit makes a nice treat. Apples, oranges, and bananas are all easy to eat. Let's take some chips and cookies, too. Oh, don't forget to bring drinks along for when we start to get thirsty.

A ball to play catch with might be a good idea, too. If it is breezy, we can fly a kite. Let's take a music player. We can dance to our favorite tunes.

With tasty food and fun things to do, we are sure to have fun!

STRATEGY PRACTICE What does the third paragraph tell you about?

_____

SKILL PRACTICE Read the question. Fill in the bubble next to the correct answer.

1. What is the passage about?
   - Ⓐ cleaning up after a picnic
   - Ⓑ getting ready for a picnic
   - Ⓒ playing a game at a picnic
   - Ⓓ flying a kite at a picnic

2. The passage says that sandwiches are good to bring because they _____.
   - Ⓐ make a nice treat
   - Ⓑ are easy to hold
   - Ⓒ are good for your body
   - Ⓓ make your friends happy

3. What is the last thing the passage says you might want to bring to the picnic?
   - Ⓐ a music player
   - Ⓑ drinks
   - Ⓒ a kite
   - Ⓓ a blanket

4. Which sentence from the passage is a fact?
   - Ⓐ "A blanket to sit on would be good."
   - Ⓑ "Sandwiches are good for picnics."
   - Ⓒ "Fruit makes a nice treat."
   - Ⓓ "If it is breezy, we can fly a kite."

READ THE PASSAGE Think about how each kind of car is different from the other.

Gas Cars or Electric Cars?

Most cars run on gasoline, or "gas" for short. Gas cars work very well. There is a problem, though. Cars that run on gas make the air dirty. This dirty air is not good for people, animals, or trees. Gas cars make the air dirty for all living things. What can we do? We can drive electric cars!

Electric cars do not use gas. These cars do not make the air dirty. These cars have battery packs that power their motors. The batteries can be charged many times. They can be used again and again. This makes electric cars great.

But electric cars have problems, too. They are slower than gas cars. They are also very quiet. This means that some people cannot hear them when they drive by. These people may not think a car is coming. They have to be careful.

People are finding ways to make electric cars better all the time. Maybe someday all cars will be electric. That would be much better for the world.

STRATEGY PRACTICE Which paragraph tells you about the problems of electric cars?

_____

SKILL PRACTICE Read the question. Fill in the bubble next to the correct answer.

1. What is the passage about?
   - Ⓐ people who ride bikes
   - Ⓑ cars that do not use gas
   - Ⓒ cars that are good for trees
   - Ⓓ people who do not need cars

2. Gas cars are bad for living things because they _____.
   - Ⓐ make the air dirty
   - Ⓑ are hard to hear
   - Ⓒ have battery packs
   - Ⓓ are slower than electric cars

3. Which of these is a fact about electric cars?
   - Ⓐ Electric cars never have problems.
   - Ⓑ Electric cars use batteries.
   - Ⓒ Electric cars are better for the world.
   - Ⓓ Batteries make electric cars great.

4. Which of these is an opinion?
   - Ⓐ Most cars run on gas.
   - Ⓑ People need cars.
   - Ⓒ Electric cars are slower than gas cars.
   - Ⓓ Electric cars are quieter than gas cars.

READ THE PASSAGE   Think about the steps a seed goes through as it grows.

What a Seed Needs

Seeds need some of the same things that we need. They need food, water, air, and sunshine. They need room to grow. They also need time to grow. If the tiny seed gets what it needs, it will grow into a plant.

Slowly, the seed sends a root down into the soil. This root pulls water up to the seed. It works like a straw. Next, the seed will slowly push up a tiny green shoot. That shoot will break through the ground. You will see it peeking through the soil.

Then, the shoot will begin to grow leaves. The new plant is called a seedling. It will grow into a bigger plant. Then, flowers will grow on the plant's stems. The flowers will open. The flowers will be very pretty.

The flowers will make new seeds. The seeds will fall to the ground and start to grow. Soon they will push up through the ground. They will become new plants!

STRATEGY PRACTICE   Does the passage tell how a seed grows into a plant or how a plant becomes a seed?

_____

SKILL PRACTICE   Read the question. Fill in the bubble next to the correct answer.

1. **What is the passage about?**
   - Ⓐ how seeds grow
   - Ⓑ birds that eat seeds
   - Ⓒ children who plant seeds
   - Ⓓ people who grow flowers

2. **Why does a seed need time?**
   - Ⓐ to get older
   - Ⓑ to get food
   - Ⓒ to make a straw
   - Ⓓ to grow

3. **What happens after a shoot comes up?**
   - Ⓐ It drops seeds.
   - Ⓑ It grows leaves.
   - Ⓒ It grows shoots.
   - Ⓓ It drops flowers.

4. **Which sentence is an opinion?**
   - Ⓐ A seed needs time to grow.
   - Ⓑ The new plant is called a seedling.
   - Ⓒ The flowers are very pretty.
   - Ⓓ The seeds will start to grow.

READ THE PASSAGE Think about the stages of a butterfly's life.

A butterfly starts its life as a tiny egg on a leaf. It hatches into a little green caterpillar. The caterpillar eats and eats. It eats milkweed leaves. The caterpillar eats and grows for two weeks. It grows into a fat, fuzzy caterpillar.

When the caterpillar stops eating, it finds a safe place to rest. It sticks itself to a leaf. Then it curls up to rest. It forms a sack, or cocoon, around itself. The caterpillar goes to sleep inside the cocoon.

The caterpillar stays in its cocoon for about ten days. Its whole body changes. When it wakes up, it is not a caterpillar anymore. In the cocoon, the caterpillar turned into a butterfly!

The butterfly unfolds its wings. The wings are orange and black. They are very beautiful. The butterfly stretches its wings. They are wet and can tear easily. The butterfly lets them dry in the sun. The wings become strong and straight. Then the butterfly flies away to find some flower nectar to drink.

STRATEGY PRACTICE Draw a star next to each paragraph that tells about caterpillars.

Which paragraph does not tell about a caterpillar? _____

SKILL PRACTICE Read the question. Fill in the bubble next to the correct answer.

1. What is the best title for the passage?
   Ⓐ "A Big Change"
   Ⓑ "A Little Green Worm"
   Ⓒ "Colorful Wings"
   Ⓓ "A Long Sleep"

2. Why does a butterfly stretch its wings?
   Ⓐ to lay an egg
   Ⓑ to form a sack
   Ⓒ to dry itself
   Ⓓ to find a flower

3. After the caterpillar eats leaves and grows, it _____.
   Ⓐ flies away
   Ⓑ sticks to a leaf
   Ⓒ curls up to sleep
   Ⓓ unfolds its wings

4. Which sentence is an opinion?
   Ⓐ The tiny egg hatches into a little green caterpillar.
   Ⓑ The caterpillar eats milkweed leaves.
   Ⓒ The caterpillar stays in its cocoon for about ten days.
   Ⓓ Butterfly wings are very beautiful.

READ THE PASSAGE Notice the order in which the speaker and Grandma do things.

Apple Pie

I love to visit Grandma. Grandma has an apple tree. When the apples are ripe, we pick some. We lean a ladder against the tree. I climb up the ladder while Grandma holds a basket below. I pick apples and hand them to Grandma.

We carry the basket into the kitchen and rinse the apples. Then we sit at Grandma's table to peel and slice the apples. We talk while we work. I tell Grandma about school and my friends. She tells me stories about when she was young. Some of her stories are funny.

I watch Grandma make the crust. She rolls the dough very thin. Then she lays it in a pan. Next, we add the apples. We add sugar and cinnamon, too. Grandma puts the top crust over them. We make marks on the top. They look pretty.

Into the oven goes our pie. I can hardly wait to taste it. Then Grandpa walks into the kitchen. "What smells so good?" Grandpa asks.

"Wait and see!" I say.

STRATEGY PRACTICE Does the passage tell about what happens first, next, and last, or does it give lots of details about one idea?

SKILL PRACTICE Read the question. Fill in the bubble next to the correct answer.

1. **What is the passage about?**
   - Ⓐ baking a pie
   - Ⓑ canning fruit
   - Ⓒ telling stories
   - Ⓓ climbing trees

2. **Why does the child climb a ladder?**
   - Ⓐ to see far and wide
   - Ⓑ to listen to stories
   - Ⓒ to talk about friends
   - Ⓓ to reach the apples

3. **What does Grandma do after she rolls the dough?**
   - Ⓐ lays it in a pan
   - Ⓑ puts it in a basket
   - Ⓒ washes it in the sink
   - Ⓓ takes it from the oven

4. **Which sentence is a fact?**
   - Ⓐ The kitchen smells nice.
   - Ⓑ We talk while we work.
   - Ⓒ Some of her stories are funny.
   - Ⓓ The marks on the crust look pretty.

Determine Important Information

When readers determine important information, they identify the type of text they are reading and then concentrate on finding the essential ideas, events, or details from that text. For nonfiction, determining importance often means finding the main idea. For fiction, it means understanding important plot points or character actions.

DAY 1

Explain to students that this week's strategy is called *Determine Important Information*. Say: **As good readers, we look for the most important information. The main idea of a passage or the topic of a chart are examples of important information. By concentrating on the most important things the writer is trying to say, we can understand better what we are reading.** Read the instructions at the top of the page aloud. Allow time for students to study the chart. Discuss with students which part or parts of the chart are most important. Complete the activities together.

DAY 2

Remind students of the strategy, and then model it by saying: **I notice that the writer has numbered some of the sentences in this passage. These are numbered directions. They are important things to look at, so I will pay close attention as I read each numbered direction.** Read the passage and complete the activities together. Optional: Have students follow the directions to create a self-portrait. After the experience, discuss how the numbered directions helped them to concentrate on one important step at a time.

DAY 3

Remind students of the strategy, and read the instructions at the top of the page aloud. Ask: **Have you seen a table of contents before? Where? What is the reason for a table of contents?** (lists parts of the book; gives page numbers of main sections; helps readers to find specific parts) **What do you notice when you look at this table of contents?** (names of animals; page numbers) Guide students through the table of contents and complete the activities together.

DAY 4

Remind students of the strategy, and read the instructions at the top of the page aloud. Read the first paragraph aloud to students, and then model the strategy: **The important thing I learned is that some dangerous trees needed to be cut down. As we read each of the other paragraphs, ask yourself which idea is the most important.** Read the passage, stopping after each paragraph to allow students to tell what the important idea is. If necessary, model appropriate responses (a worker found baby owls in one tree; they did not cut down the tree until the owls grew up and flew away). Complete the activities together.

DAY 5

Remind students of the strategy, and read the instructions at the top of the page aloud. Say: **Sometimes the best way to give information is in a chart or graph. Let's read the words on the graph and look at it carefully. We will want to think about what important information is being shown.** Discuss the graph and complete the activities together.

READ THE CHART Decide what kind of chart this is.

SUNDAY	MONDAY	TUESDAY	WEDNESDAY	THURSDAY	FRIDAY	SATURDAY
SUNNY	SUNNY	PARTLY CLOUDY	PARTLY CLOUDY	CLOUDY	RAINY	WINDY

STRATEGY PRACTICE Complete the sentence.

This chart tells me about _weather_ .

SKILL PRACTICE Read the question. Fill in the bubble next to the correct answer.

1. What is the best title for the chart?
   Ⓐ "Math Facts We Know"
   Ⓑ "School Lunch Menu"
   Ⓒ "This Week's Weather"
   Ⓓ "Weekly Spelling Words"

2. What will the weather be like on Monday?
   Ⓐ sunny
   Ⓑ cloudy
   Ⓒ rainy
   Ⓓ windy

3. What do the words at the top of the chart tell?
   Ⓐ months of the year
   Ⓑ times of the day
   Ⓒ words in a book
   Ⓓ days of the week

4. On the last day, the weather will be _____.
   Ⓐ cloudy with some sun
   Ⓑ windy
   Ⓒ rainy
   Ⓓ sunny

Think about each step talked about in the passage.

How to Draw Yourself

To draw yourself, you will need a mirror, a big piece of paper, and crayons. Now follow these steps:

1. Look in the mirror. What is the shape of your head? It is oval like an egg.

2. Draw a large oval on your piece of paper. Leave room at the top for your hair. Leave room at the bottom for your neck and shoulders.

3. Look at your eyes in the mirror. What color are they? How are they shaped?

4. Draw your eyes and eyebrows.

5. Look at your ears. Their tops are even with your eyes. They go down to the bottom of your nose.

6. Add your ears and nose to the picture.

7. Look at your mouth in the mirror. How wide is it? How is it shaped?

8. Add your mouth, neck, and shoulders to the picture.

9. Now draw some hair on your head. This will make you look much better.

See how great you look! There is only one you.

STRATEGY PRACTICE Underline all the things the passage tells you to draw.

SKILL PRACTICE Read the question. Fill in the bubble next to the correct answer.

1. The passage tells you how to _____.
   Ⓐ pick a hat
   Ⓑ draw a tree
   Ⓒ cut your hair
   Ⓓ draw a picture

2. Which one of these is drawn first?
   Ⓐ nose
   Ⓑ eyes
   Ⓒ ears
   Ⓓ mouth

3. What does the passage tell you to do before you draw your head?
   Ⓐ Look at yourself.
   Ⓑ Look at your ears.
   Ⓒ Draw grass and trees.
   Ⓓ Draw a mouth and a neck.

4. In which step do you draw your neck?
   Ⓐ step 4
   Ⓑ step 2
   Ⓒ step 8
   Ⓓ step 9

READ THE TABLE OF CONTENTS Think about what the table of contents tells you.

Table of Contents

Bears 1

Elephants 4

Lions 7

Monkeys 10

Wild Birds.. 13

Zebras 16

STRATEGY PRACTICE Complete the sentence.

A table of contents helps a reader to _____.

SKILL PRACTICE Read the question. Fill in the bubble next to the correct answer.

1. The table of contents is from which of these books?

   Ⓐ "At My House"

   Ⓑ "At the Zoo"

   Ⓒ "In My School"

   Ⓓ "At the Store"

2. On which page would you read about animals that fly?

   Ⓐ page 4

   Ⓑ page 7

   Ⓒ page 10

   Ⓓ page 13

3. The part about monkeys begins on page _____.

   Ⓐ 4

   Ⓑ 7

   Ⓒ 10

   Ⓓ 13

4. What animal will you read about first?

   Ⓐ bears

   Ⓑ lions

   Ⓒ birds

   Ⓓ elephants

READ THE PASSAGE   Look for the most important ideas.

Last year in California, a team of tree cutters were sent to a job. A row of tall trees along a city road needed to be cut down. The trees were beautiful, but they were sick. They were dropping big branches. The branches were dangerous for cars on the road below.

The workers started to cut down the trees. They cut down the first tree. They cut down the second and third trees. Then a worker climbed the fourth tree to cut off its lowest branch. He saw something surprising. Tucked into a hole in the tree were five baby barn owls!

The worker climbed down the tree. He told the other workers about the baby owls. They cut down the other trees. They did not cut down the tree that had the baby owls in it. They waited. They waited until the owls were older. They did not cut down the tree until the owls flew away.

STRATEGY PRACTICE   Underline one sentence in each paragraph that you think is the most important of the paragraph.

SKILL PRACTICE   Read the question. Fill in the bubble next to the correct answer.

1. **Which one would be a good title for the passage?**

Ⓐ "All About Owls"

Ⓑ "How to Cut Down Trees"

Ⓒ "Dangerous Trees"

Ⓓ "The Owls and the Tree Cutter"

2. **The tree cutter sees the owls before _____.**

Ⓐ the trees are sick

Ⓑ the owls can fly

Ⓒ the cutters go to the job

Ⓓ the workers cut down any trees

3. **After the worker sees the baby owls, he _____.**

Ⓐ builds a new nest

Ⓑ cuts down the tree

Ⓒ tells the other workers

Ⓓ drops some big branches

4. **What do the workers do after the owls fly away?**

Ⓐ cut down the last tree

Ⓑ leave the last tree standing

Ⓒ call a doctor for the last tree

Ⓓ wait for the last tree to grow

READ THE GRAPH   Look carefully at each part of the bar graph.

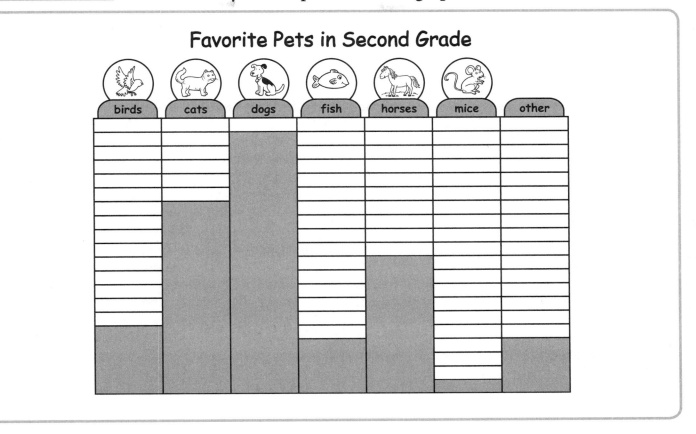

STRATEGY PRACTICE   Complete the sentence.

The graph tells about _____.

SKILL PRACTICE   Read the question. Fill in the bubble next to the correct answer.

1. The words at the top of the graph name different _____.

   Ⓐ animals

   Ⓑ books

   Ⓒ schools

   Ⓓ teachers

2. What does the graph show after "fish"?

   Ⓐ cats

   Ⓑ dogs

   Ⓒ birds

   Ⓓ horses

3. Which pet was picked the most?

   Ⓐ cats

   Ⓑ birds

   Ⓒ dogs

   Ⓓ horses

4. Which is the least favorite pet?

   Ⓐ birds

   Ⓑ mice

   Ⓒ fish

   Ⓓ horses

Ask Questions

By asking questions, readers can set a purpose for reading or make sure they understood what they have read. Good readers ask questions to involve themselves with the text and often ask questions before, during, and after they read.

DAY 1

Tell students that this week they will learn how to ask questions to help them as they read. Say: **Good readers often ask questions before they read something. This helps to set a purpose for reading. Good readers also look at the title to see what the passage is about. Then they ask themselves questions about the topic that they want to find the answers to.** Read the title of the passage aloud. List on the board questions for which students want to find answers. Have them choose a question and write it in the space provided for the strategy practice activity. Then read aloud the instructions at the top of the page. Read the passage together, and then invite volunteers to share their questions and discuss how it helped them set a purpose for reading. Complete the second activity together.

DAY 2

Remind students of the strategy. Say: **Asking questions as we read is a good way to check our understanding. Asking questions while we read helps us get more involved in the text and notice information that we don't understand.** Read the instructions at the top of the page aloud. Read the story together, stopping after each paragraph to allow students to ask questions they have about the passage. If students don't volunteer questions, be prepared with some of your own (e.g., *Why didn't the father do anything when his sons fought? What's the father going to do with the sticks?*) Allow time for students to complete the first activity and share responses. Complete the second activity together.

DAY 3

Remind students of the strategy. Say: **Asking questions after we read helps us check that we understood what we read. We ask ourselves or each other the kinds of questions that our textbooks would ask.** Read the instructions at the top of the page aloud, and then read the story together. Then model asking a question based on information from the passage: **What happens at Dana's house when it snows?** Allow time for students to complete the strategy practice activity. Invite partners to share their questions and answers. Complete the second activity together.

DAY 4

Remind students of the strategy. Tell students they will be reading a passage about a boy who can do something unusual. Say: **Sometimes we can ask questions to get more involved in a story and enjoy it more.** Read the instructions at the top of the page aloud, and then read the passage together. When students have finished reading, model using the strategy. Say: **When I read about Dion lifting off the ground, I tried to imagine what that would feel like. I brought myself deeper into their story.** Direct students to complete the strategy practice activity. Invite volunteers to share their responses and explain their thinking behind the questions they wrote. Then direct students to complete the skill practice activity. Review the answers together.

DAY 5

Remind students of the strategy. Tell them they will be reading a well-known folk tale from Japan that has some unusual happenings. Read the instructions at the top of the page aloud, and then read the story together. Invite students to think of questions about the passage. Write the questions on the board. Direct students to choose a question and write it in the space provided for the strategy practice activity. Then have partners answer each other's questions. Complete the skill practice activity together.

READ THE PASSAGE Think of questions you have about the Statue of Liberty.

The Statue of Liberty

The Statue of Liberty stands on a small island in New York Harbor. People who come to this country on ships see Lady Liberty standing there. She welcomes them at the end of their long trip across the sea. The statue holds a torch high above her head. The torch stands for freedom.

France gave the statue to our country as a gift of friendship. It was made in France. It came across the ocean in pieces. Then it was put together here.

The statue is made of copper and steel. It is as tall as a building with 30 floors. The statue's face is very big. The nose is as long as your body. The fingers are about as long as the ceiling in a room is high!

There are stairs inside of the statue. People climb 354 steps to get to the crown. Thirty people can fit in the crown. There are 25 windows in it. They can see the ships that the statue is welcoming.

STRATEGY PRACTICE A question I want to find the answer to is:

_____

SKILL PRACTICE Read the question. Fill in the bubble next to the correct answer.

1. The passage is about _____.
   - Ⓐ visiting New York
   - Ⓑ taking a trip on a ship
   - Ⓒ a famous statue
   - Ⓓ climbing up stairs

2. How is the Statue of Liberty different from a person?
   - Ⓐ It can hold a torch.
   - Ⓑ It has a nose.
   - Ⓒ It is made of copper and steel.
   - Ⓓ It has hands and fingers.

3. One way the statue is like a person is that it _____.
   - Ⓐ has stairs inside of it
   - Ⓑ has eyes and a nose
   - Ⓒ is as tall as a building
   - Ⓓ is made of copper and steel

4. The author most likely wrote the passage to tell _____.
   - Ⓐ a story about a funny woman
   - Ⓑ about what is made in France
   - Ⓒ about a crown you can stand in
   - Ⓓ about something important in our country

READ THE PASSAGE After each paragraph, think of a question you have.

There once lived an old man who had five sons. The young men did not get along with each other. They fought about who would milk the cow. They fought over who would ride the fastest horse. They fought with each other all day long.

The man was sad to see his sons fight. He called them together. He was holding a bundle of sticks.

"I want you to break this bundle of sticks," the man told his sons.

Each son took his turn. Each tried with all his might to break the bundle of sticks. None of them could do it.

Then the father untied the bundle. He handed each son a stick. "Now try to break the sticks," he said. They did so very easily.

"You are like these sticks," the man said. "You are weak if you stand alone. You are strong if you work together."

STRATEGY PRACTICE Write one question you asked while you were reading.

_____

SKILL PRACTICE Read the question. Fill in the bubble next to the correct answer.

1. **What is the best title for the passage?**
   - Ⓐ "Riding a Horse"
   - Ⓑ "Milking a Cow"
   - Ⓒ "The Bundle of Sticks"
   - Ⓓ "Boys and Their Father"

2. **How are the brothers alike?**
   - Ⓐ They are all fast riders.
   - Ⓑ They can break bundles of sticks.
   - Ⓒ They all fight one another.
   - Ⓓ They all make their father proud.

3. **How are the brothers the same as the sticks?**
   - Ⓐ They are all broken.
   - Ⓑ They are all the same.
   - Ⓒ They are in a bundle.
   - Ⓓ They are stronger together.

4. **The author most likely wrote the passage to _____.**
   - Ⓐ teach a lesson
   - Ⓑ make people laugh
   - Ⓒ tell how to milk cows
   - Ⓓ show how to break sticks

READ THE PASSAGE Ask yourself what you know about the home being described.

Island Home, Mountain Home

My name is Juan. I live on an island. My house is made of wood. It sits on top of long, strong poles that go deep into the sand. When storms hit the shore, the water rushes right under my house!

The air is warm where I live. I wear shorts and a T-shirt. I wear a hat to keep the sun off my face. My older brother and I sail our little boat on the sea. We catch many fish. Our mother cooks them for dinner.

My name is Dana. I live in the mountains. My family and I live in a home made of pine tree logs. When it snows, my father shovels a path from our door to the road. The snow on the sides of the path piles up so high that it is above my head!

I wear a jacket in the winter. I wear a hat and gloves, too. In the summer, my brother and I pick berries. We bake a berry pie.

STRATEGY PRACTICE Write a question about the passage. Have a partner answer it.

_____

SKILL PRACTICE Read the question. Fill in the bubble next to the correct answer.

1. **What is the passage about?**
   Ⓐ different places people live
   Ⓑ what mountains look like
   Ⓒ how to catch fish in the sea
   Ⓓ places that are warm all the time

2. **How is Juan's home the same as Dana's?**
   Ⓐ It is by the water.
   Ⓑ It sits on poles.
   Ⓒ It is made of wood.
   Ⓓ Water rushes under it.

3. **One way Juan and Dana are the same is that they both _____.**
   Ⓐ sail boats
   Ⓑ pick berries
   Ⓒ wear gloves
   Ⓓ have brothers

4. **Why did the author write the passage?**
   Ⓐ to teach you how to catch fish
   Ⓑ to tell you about two places where people live
   Ⓒ to persuade you to move to a new place
   Ⓓ to entertain you with a story about kids

READ THE PASSAGE Ask yourself which parts could be real and which could not.

"Come watch me, Mom! I'm flying!" She followed me to the backyard.

I climbed up onto the picnic table. I put my arms out. I jumped away from the table as far as I could.

I landed on the grass. "Did you see that, Mom?" I asked. "I flew a little bit."

"Hmm. Maybe a little, Dion," she said. I could tell that she didn't really think so.

The next day after school, I was playing football with a boy named Hector. I caught the ball and ran. Hector ran after me. I ran across the field toward the goal. Hector was right behind me. He was getting closer.

Just then, my feet slowly left the ground. I kept running, but soon I was running up through the air!

I landed on the roof of the school and turned around to look down. Hector was standing below with his mouth wide open like a fish.

"That doesn't count!" Hector yelled. "You are out of bounds. It's my turn now."

STRATEGY PRACTICE Write a question that helped you enjoy the passage more.

_____

_____

SKILL PRACTICE Read the question. Fill in the bubble next to the correct answer.

1. **What is the best title for the passage?**
   - Ⓐ "Play Ball!"
   - Ⓑ "I Can Fly!"
   - Ⓒ "On the Roof"
   - Ⓓ "A Good Game"

2. **Which of these could not happen?**
   - Ⓐ Dion lands on the grass.
   - Ⓑ Hector chases Dion.
   - Ⓒ Hector opens his mouth wide.
   - Ⓓ Dion runs through the air.

3. **What can Dion do that Hector cannot?**
   - Ⓐ fly up to a roof
   - Ⓑ take a turn
   - Ⓒ run across a field
   - Ⓓ jump from a table

4. **The author most likely wanted to _____.**
   - Ⓐ show how to jump
   - Ⓑ show how to play football
   - Ⓒ tell a funny story
   - Ⓓ tell how to fly

READ THE PASSAGE   Ask yourself what is real and what is fantasy.

Long ago and far away, there lived an old man and woman. One day, the woman was washing clothes in the river. A great big peach floated to her. She took the peach home to eat.

When the woman began to open the peach, out jumped a little boy! The man and woman named him Momotaro, or Peach Boy. He grew up strong and brave.

Life was wonderful until some ogres moved onto a nearby island. The ogres were stealing from the people. Momotaro wanted to make them go away.

So Momotaro packed some of his mother's tasty dumplings. Along the way, he met a dog, a monkey, and a bird. Momotaro gave them each a dumpling. Each one said, "I will help you get rid of the ogres."

With the help of his three friends, Momotaro made the ogres go away. Momotaro and his friends returned home with the ogre's treasure. Everyone in the town cheered and called him a hero.

STRATEGY PRACTICE   Write a question you have about the passage. Have a partner answer it.

_____

SKILL PRACTICE   Read the question. Fill in the bubble next to the correct answer.

1. **Which one is the best title for the passage?**
   Ⓐ "The Long River"
   Ⓑ "The Sweet Fruit"
   Ⓒ "A Special Son"
   Ⓓ "The Helpful Animals"

2. **Which of these is real?**
   Ⓐ animals that talk
   Ⓑ a woman who washes clothes
   Ⓒ a boy who comes out of a peach
   Ⓓ ogres on an island

3. **How is Momotaro different from a real person?**
   Ⓐ Momotaro can eat dumplings.
   Ⓑ Momotaro came from a peach.
   Ⓒ Momotaro is brave.
   Ⓓ Momotaro has animal friends.

4. **The author most likely wrote the passage to tell _____.**
   Ⓐ how helpful animals are
   Ⓑ how to get rid of ogres
   Ⓒ how a peach can be a boy
   Ⓓ an interesting, make-believe tale

Monitor Comprehension

When students monitor their comprehension, they keep track of how well they understand the material and identify when their understanding breaks down. Related activities include asking questions, underlining important ideas, and paraphrasing what they have read.

DAY 1

Tell students that this week's strategy is called *Monitor Comprehension.* Say: **When you monitor your comprehension, you pay attention to how well you understand what you are reading.** Read the instructions at the top of the page, the title, and the first paragraph of the passage aloud to students. Then model the strategy: **When I read the title, I thought about lots of things that could be under the waves. I wondered which one the passage was going to be about. When I read the first sentence, I found out that the passage was about submarines. I stopped after I read the rest of the first paragraph and asked myself what I remembered. I monitored my comprehension.** Have students read the first paragraph, and then ask them to share what they remember. Repeat this process for the remaining paragraphs, reminding students that they are monitoring their comprehension. Direct students to complete the first activity and share their responses. Then complete the second activity together.

DAY 2

Remind students of the strategy, and read the instructions at the top of the page aloud. Ask: **How will finding out if you agree with Jamie's mother help you monitor your comprehension?** (You will have to remember what she said and what happened in the story to know if you agree or disagree.) After students finish reading, write responses to the first activity on the board. Allow students to copy the response of their choice. Then complete the second activity together.

DAY 3

Remind students of the strategy, and read the instructions at the top of the page aloud. Explain: **When you monitor your comprehension, you can use other strategies that we have practiced. As you read this passage, you will make connections to help you monitor your comprehension. You will think about how the parties you are reading about are the same or different from parties you have been to.** After reading the passage, complete the activities together.

DAY 4

Remind students of the strategy, and read the instructions at the top of the page aloud. Ask: **What other strategy do you think you'll be using to help you monitor your comprehension when you read this passage?** (*Visualization,* or making a mental picture) Remind students that when they make mental pictures, they use describing words, or adjectives, to help them "see" what they are reading about. After reading the passage, complete the activities together.

DAY 5

Remind students of the strategy, and read the instructions at the top of the page aloud. Explain: **Today you will monitor your comprehension by finding and remembering something about ants.** List questions students have on the board before reading the passage. After reading, monitor comprehension by seeing which of the students' questions can be answered. Complete the activities together.

READ THE PASSAGE   Stop at the end of each paragraph. What do you remember?

Under the Waves

Have you ever wondered how it feels to ride in a submarine? This kind of boat can go under the water. The captain makes it go left or right. He makes it go up and down. Some submarines can dive down to the bottom of the sea.

There are many kinds of submarines. Some are very big. Others are small. Some have tall windows for people to look through.

People who ride in submarines can see many beautiful things. They see bright coral with colors like jelly beans. They see tiny, shiny fish swimming around the coral. They see great sea animals like whales. They see sharks and eels.

It is safe inside the submarine. There is enough air for the people to breathe. The air is not too warm or too cold. The people inside have food to eat. Those who go on long trips even have places to sleep!

Submarines help us to learn about the wonders of the sea. They show us parts of the sea that other boats cannot.

STRATEGY PRACTICE   Tell a partner three things you remember about submarines.

SKILL PRACTICE   Read the question. Fill in the bubble next to the correct answer.

1. What does the title tell you about submarines?
   - Ⓐ where they go
   - Ⓑ how they move
   - Ⓒ who rides in them
   - Ⓓ what they look like

2. What is true about submarines?
   - Ⓐ People ride in submarines.
   - Ⓑ Submarines catch whales.
   - Ⓒ Submarines are all the same size.
   - Ⓓ Submarines are filled with cold air.

3. Which one tells that coral is pretty?
   - Ⓐ It lives in the sea.
   - Ⓑ It grows in groups.
   - Ⓒ It has bright colors.
   - Ⓓ It is looked at by people.

4. The passage is about a kind of _____.
   - Ⓐ bed
   - Ⓑ boat
   - Ⓒ fish
   - Ⓓ food

READ THE PASSAGE   Ask yourself if you agree with what Jamie's mother says.

Try and Try Again

Boing! The basketball bounced off the rim of the hoop.

"I almost made it that time," Jamie said. She looked at the hoop and threw the ball. It flew way over the hoop and landed on the neighbor's lawn.

The sun was hot on the driveway. Jamie wiped her forehead.

Jamie's mother saw her through the kitchen window. She saw that Jamie looked sad. "Do you want some lemonade?" she called.

"Yes, please," Jamie answered. She felt tired. The lemonade was cold and sweet. "I'll never make a basket!" Jamie moaned.

"Keep trying, honey," her mother said. "If you keep trying, you will do it."

Back on the driveway, Jamie tried again. "I can do it," she said to herself. She held up the ball and looked at the basket for a very long minute. She threw the ball. Up, up it went. It tapped the rim and then slowly rolled through the hoop.

"I did it!" Jamie shouted and clapped. "I made a basket at last!"

STRATEGY PRACTICE   Circle the word or words, and complete the sentence.

I (do   do not) agree with Jamie's mother because _____.

SKILL PRACTICE   Read the question. Fill in the bubble next to the correct answer.

1. What is the passage about?
   Ⓐ a girl playing basketball
   Ⓑ a neighbor's lawn
   Ⓒ a mother making lemonade
   Ⓓ a hot driveway

2. Which one tells that Jamie feels hot?
   Ⓐ She claps and jumps.
   Ⓑ She calls her mother.
   Ⓒ She looks at the basket.
   Ⓓ She wipes her forehead.

3. What do you think will happen next?
   Ⓐ The ball will pop.
   Ⓑ The ball will get lost.
   Ⓒ Jamie will make another basket.
   Ⓓ Jamie will make lemonade.

4. What does the title tell you?
   Ⓐ what Jamie says
   Ⓑ what Jamie does
   Ⓒ how Jamie feels
   Ⓓ how Jamie looks

READ THE PASSAGE Think about how parties you have been to are the same or different.

Party Time

A birthday party is a lot of fun. Some parties are big and have many people. Some parties are small. People like to go to parties. What will you find when you get there? Most birthday parties have good food, nice music, and fun games.

Food

Popcorn, ice cream, and pizza are some of the foods found at many parties. So is birthday cake! Eating together is one way that people enjoy the party.

Music

Many birthday parties have music. Some have dancing, too. Many people sing "Happy Birthday."

Games

People love to play games. A fun game is called "Pin the Tail on the Donkey." Players take turns wearing a blindfold. They stick a paper tail on a picture of a donkey. The tail lands in funny places. Everyone laughs and has fun.

STRATEGY PRACTICE Complete the sentence.

One different food I have had at a party is _____.

SKILL PRACTICE Read the question. Fill in the bubble next to the correct answer.

1. The passage is about _____.
   Ⓐ who goes to parties
   Ⓑ what happens at parties
   Ⓒ what people buy for parties
   Ⓓ what people wear to parties

2. Which party food does the passage mention?
   Ⓐ ice cubes
   Ⓑ creamed corn
   Ⓒ birthday cake
   Ⓓ peas

3. If someone brings out a birthday cake, what will probably happen next?
   Ⓐ People will go home.
   Ⓑ People will play a game.
   Ⓒ People will eat pizza.
   Ⓓ People will sing "Happy Birthday."

4. What do the headings tell?
   Ⓐ what parties have
   Ⓑ where parties are
   Ⓒ when parties start
   Ⓓ why parties happen

READ THE PASSAGE Picture what a coconut looks like.

A coconut is a great big seed. It does not look like much on the outside. It is round and brown. It seems like a strange kind of ball. But the coconut is full of surprises. It is used in many different ways.

The little hairs on the outside of a coconut are used to make rope, sacks, and doormats. People use the shells to make bowls and buttons. They also burn these shells to help keep bugs away! Oil from the nuts is used for cooking. It is also used to make soap.

A coconut is hard to open. It is hollow on the inside. It is filled with sweet water. This water is good to drink. The inside wall of the coconut is white like snow. It is very good to eat. It is used to make pies and other treats. The palm tree that coconuts grow on is useful, too. People make brooms and baskets from different parts of the leaves.

Coconut palms use the sea to spread their seeds. The nuts float across the water. The seeds grow into new trees on land far away.

STRATEGY PRACTICE Underline words in the passage that describe what a coconut looks like.

SKILL PRACTICE Read the question. Fill in the bubble next to the correct answer.

1. Which title goes best with the passage?
   Ⓐ "The Coconut Pie"
   Ⓑ "The Coconut Leaf"
   Ⓒ "The Round Coconut"
   Ⓓ "The Useful Coconut"

2. What is true about coconuts?
   Ⓐ They fly on the wind.
   Ⓑ They make good bowls.
   Ⓒ They feel cold like snow.
   Ⓓ They make good footballs.

3. Which one tells that palm leaves are useful for cleaning?
   Ⓐ Some become brooms.
   Ⓑ Some fall from the trees.
   Ⓒ They have different parts.
   Ⓓ They grow with coconuts.

4. Which of these will happen if you plant a coconut?
   Ⓐ A tree will grow.
   Ⓑ More nuts will come up.
   Ⓒ It will float away.
   Ⓓ A squirrel will eat it.

READ THE PASSAGE As you read, think about something you learn about ants.

Teamwork

Ants can do all kinds of work. Some find food. Others carry it. Some dig nests. Some ants work to keep the nest safe. Others keep it clean. Ants take care of their eggs. They feed their babies. Ants can do these things and more because they work in teams.

Ants leave trails that the others can smell. They leave trails to lead other ants to food. If a path is blocked, ants leave trails to show the others where to go. They also leave trails that tell other ants that a place is no longer safe.

Some people do not like ants. If ants come into your house and your parents do not like it, try this trick. Put a little bit of sugar outside. The ants will be busy with the sugar. They will stop looking for food in your house. The ants will be happy. Your parents will be happy, too!

STRATEGY PRACTICE Write one thing you learned about ants.

_____

SKILL PRACTICE Read the question. Fill in the bubble next to the correct answer.

1. **What does the title tell you about ants?**

   Ⓐ They play sports.

   Ⓑ They choose sides.

   Ⓒ They have numbers.

   Ⓓ They work together.

2. **You can keep ants from coming into your house by _____.**

   Ⓐ blocking their trails

   Ⓑ putting sugar outside

   Ⓒ moving their parents

   Ⓓ digging new ant nests

3. **Which one tells that ants help each other to be safe?**

   Ⓐ They show where danger is.

   Ⓑ They take care of their eggs.

   Ⓒ They look for food in houses.

   Ⓓ They smell trails left by others.

4. **What is true about the ants in the passage?**

   Ⓐ They work alone.

   Ⓑ They follow people.

   Ⓒ They clean their homes.

   Ⓓ They build nests in trees.

Main Idea and Details

Students look for the central idea or message of a passage or story. They also find details that best support the main idea.

Sequence

Students look for the order of events or steps in a process.

DAY 1

Introduce the *Main Idea and Details* skill to students. Say: **Good readers want to understand what a passage is mostly about. They look for the main idea. Ideas that tell us more about the main idea are called** *details.* Remind students of the *Monitor Comprehension* strategy (taught during Week 6). Say: **As you read, stop to ask yourself if you know what the main idea of a paragraph is.** Read the instructions at the top of the page aloud. After students have read the passage, direct them to read the second paragraph again. Ask: **What is the paragraph mostly about?** (what the colors on the flag stand for) **Which sentence gives us an important detail about the color red?** ("Red stands for being brave and strong.") Direct students to complete the skill practice activity, and then review the answers together. After students complete the strategy practice activity, invite volunteers to share their answers.

DAY 2

Remind students of the skill, and read the instructions at the top of the page aloud. Have a student read the title aloud. Say: **A good title sometimes tells you about the main idea of a passage. When I read this title, I learn that I am going to read about crickets. I know that crickets are insects, but I wonder how a cricket is lucky. Let's read to find out.** After students read the passage, invite them to tell what they think the main idea of the passage is (Crickets are jumping insects that make a chirping sound. Some people think that crickets bring good luck.). Complete the skill practice activity and review the answers together. Remind students that good readers identify the information that is the most important. You may wish to review the *Determine Important Information* strategy (taught during Week 4). Direct students to complete the strategy practice activity, and then discuss responses, recognizing that there are more than three important sentences in the passage.

DAY 3

Introduce the *Sequence* skill to students. Say: *Sequence* **is the order in which things happen in a story or the steps for doing something.** Brainstorm with students to list times when sequence is important (following directions to get somewhere; steps in an art project or recipe; etc.). **Good readers use the** *Monitor Comprehension* **strategy to keep track of the sequence of events. A good way to monitor your comprehension when you read a fictional story is to make a mental picture of what is happening.** Read the instructions at the top of the page aloud. After students have read the passage, complete the skill practice activity together. Then have students locate answer choices in the text and underline them. Direct students to complete the strategy practice activity. Allow several students to share their responses.

DAY 4

Remind students of the *Sequence* skill. Say: **Good readers look for signal words, such as** *first, next, then,* **and** *last* **to find important steps in a process.** Read the instructions at the top of the page aloud. After students have read the passage, complete the skill practice activity and review the answers together. You may wish to review the *Determine Important Information* strategy. Direct students to complete the strategy practice activity, and then discuss responses, recognizing that there are more than three important sentences in the passage.

DAY 5

Tell students they will practice finding the main idea and important details, as well as looking for sequence in a passage. Then remind students of the *Monitor Comprehension* strategy. Read the instructions at the top of the page aloud. After students have read the passage, complete the activities and review the answers together.

 Daily Reading Comprehension • EMC 3452 • © Evan-Moor Corp.

READ THE PASSAGE   Look for the main idea of each paragraph.

Our Flag

We know the flag stands for our country. But why are there stars and stripes on our flag? Why is it red, white, and blue? What do the colors and shapes mean?

Each color on our flag has a meaning. Red stands for being brave and strong. White stands for doing what is right. It also means saying what is true. Blue stands for being fair. It also means working hard.

There are thirteen stripes on our flag. They stand for the first thirteen states. Our first flag had thirteen stars on it, too. A woman named Betsy Ross sewed it over 200 years ago. Since then, a star has been added for each state that joins the country.

There are now 50 stars on our flag. Each state has its own star. All the stars stand together. This shows that we are all joined to love and protect our country.

SKILL PRACTICE   Read the question. Fill in the bubble next to the correct answer.

1. What is the passage mostly about?
   Ⓐ 50 stars
   Ⓑ the U.S. flag
   Ⓒ colors and shapes
   Ⓓ red and white stripes

2. What did Betsy Ross do?
   Ⓐ She said what is true.
   Ⓑ She worked very hard.
   Ⓒ She saved the country.
   Ⓓ She sewed the first flag.

3. The flag's colors stand for _____.
   Ⓐ loving our country
   Ⓑ the person who made it
   Ⓒ good ways to act
   Ⓓ all the 50 states

4. Each star stands for a _____.
   Ⓐ state
   Ⓑ stripe
   Ⓒ woman
   Ⓓ country

STRATEGY PRACTICE   Tell a partner what the colors and shapes of the flag stand for.

Look for sentences that give important details about crickets.

The Lucky Cricket

The cricket is a little insect that makes a big sound. It can rub its wings together and chirp like a bird! It chirps fast when the air is warm. It chirps slowly when the air is cool.

Crickets live under rocks and logs. They are brown or black. They look a lot like grasshoppers. They can jump like grasshoppers, too. They use their back legs to jump. Some can jump three feet in the air!

Many people think that crickets bring good luck. Some think their chirps mean that money is coming soon. Others think the cricket's chirp means that it will rain.

In China, some people keep crickets as pets. They give them names. They keep them in cages. They feed them bugs, plants, and seeds. These people feel happy when their crickets chirp. They like to hear the song of luck chirping through their homes.

SKILL PRACTICE   Read the question. Fill in the bubble next to the correct answer.

1. The passage is mostly about _____.

   Ⓐ a noisy bug

   Ⓑ a cage for a pet

   Ⓒ a happy song

   Ⓓ birds chirping

2. The cricket chirps by _____.

   Ⓐ going under a rock

   Ⓑ using its legs to jump

   Ⓒ eating plants and seeds

   Ⓓ rubbing its wings together

3. Crickets look a lot like _____.

   Ⓐ rocks

   Ⓑ birds

   Ⓒ grasshoppers

   Ⓓ logs

4. Based on the passage, many people think that crickets _____.

   Ⓐ cannot be kept as pets

   Ⓑ are good to have around

   Ⓒ are too noisy

   Ⓓ are the best jumpers

STRATEGY PRACTICE   Underline three sentences that tell important ideas about crickets.

Pay attention to the order in which things happen.

The Big Catch

Ben and his dad row out onto the lake. They have jackets for later. They have sandwiches and drinks. They wear hats to protect their heads from the sun.

Now it is time to begin. First, Ben's dad strings the pole with a hook at the end of the line. Next, he puts bait on the hook. He is careful. The hook is sharp.

When the line is ready, Ben casts it. He knows a way to make the hook fly far over the water. Now Ben waits. He stays very quiet. He does not want to scare the fish away. He likes looking at the pretty trees near the lake. He likes the fresh smell of the water. He likes being with his dad.

Is that a tug Ben feels? "Wow!" Dad cries, "Turn the reel! Pull it in!"

Ben keeps turning until the fish flops onto the floor of the boat.

"It's a trout!" Dad shouts with a great big smile. They will take the fish home and cook it for dinner. It will be the best meal that Ben has ever had.

SKILL PRACTICE Read the question. Fill in the bubble next to the correct answer.

1. Which one happens first?

    Ⓐ Ben and his dad feel a tug.

    Ⓑ Ben and his dad stay quiet.

    Ⓒ Ben and his dad bait the hook.

    Ⓓ Ben and his dad string the pole.

2. Which one will happen last?

    Ⓐ Ben and his dad will eat the fish.

    Ⓑ Ben and his dad will bait the hook.

    Ⓒ Ben and his dad will go to the lake.

    Ⓓ Ben and his dad will catch the fish.

3. When does the dad smile?

    Ⓐ when they eat the fish

    Ⓑ after they catch the fish

    Ⓒ as they row onto the lake

    Ⓓ before they get on the boat

4. When does the dad string the pole?

    Ⓐ after they bait the hook

    Ⓑ after they catch the fish

    Ⓒ before they row the boat

    Ⓓ before they catch the fish

STRATEGY PRACTICE Tell a partner the steps to catch a fish in the correct order.

READ THE PASSAGE Remember the important steps in learning to swim.

Swim Lessons

Swimming is fun! It is time to learn how. What happens at a swim lesson?

First, you meet your teacher. Then, into the water you go! You will learn in the shallow end of the pool. You can stand up in the water there. Your teacher might have you start by jumping up and down in the water. Jump, jump, jump! You and the other children jump in one place. Then you jump together across the pool.

Next, the teacher might ask you to blow bubbles. The water feels cool on your face. You lift your face to take a breath, and then blow more bubbles in the water.

Kicking is a big part of swimming. Hold onto the wall and kick your legs. "Try to splash me over here!" your teacher might shout with a smile.

Every day, you will learn something new. You will learn how to float. You will learn how to move your arms. Soon, you will be able to move your arms and kick at the same time. Before you know it, you will be swimming across the pool!

SKILL PRACTICE   Read the question. Fill in the bubble next to the correct answer.

1. **What will you learn first?**
   - Ⓐ to kick your legs
   - Ⓑ to blow bubbles in the water
   - Ⓒ to jump up and down
   - Ⓓ how to move your arms

2. **What happens before you learn to kick?**
   - Ⓐ You float in the water.
   - Ⓑ You move your arms.
   - Ⓒ You swim across the pool.
   - Ⓓ You blow bubbles in the water.

3. **What would you do after you jump in one place?**
   - Ⓐ jump across the pool
   - Ⓑ stand in the shallow end
   - Ⓒ learn how to move your arms
   - Ⓓ move your arms while you kick

4. **Which one is a time order word?**
   - Ⓐ so
   - Ⓑ next
   - Ⓒ and
   - Ⓓ for

STRATEGY PRACTICE   Underline three important things you do when you learn to swim.

READ THE PASSAGE   Stop after each paragraph and tell yourself what you remember.

Sweet Honey

Do bees make honey just for us? People do like honey, but that is not why bees make it. They make it as food for themselves. It gives them the energy they need to do their busy bee work.

First, the bees collect nectar. Nectar is a clear liquid in flowers. It is mostly water. The bees have long tongues. Their tongues work like straws! The bees suck the juice from the flowers. Then, they carry it back to their nest, or hive.

Next, bees in the hive chew the nectar. This changes the sugars in it. Then, they spread it in their honeycombs.

As the nectar dries, it gets thick. To help it dry faster, the bees fan it with their wings! After it is dry and sticky, the bees close the comb. Later, the bees open the comb and eat the honey. They like it as much as we do!

SKILL PRACTICE   Read the question. Fill in the bubble next to the correct answer.

1. The passage is mostly about how bees _____.
   Ⓐ find nectar
   Ⓑ make honey
   Ⓒ build their nests
   Ⓓ move their wings

2. Where do the bees find nectar?
   Ⓐ in hives
   Ⓑ on combs
   Ⓒ on bread
   Ⓓ in flowers

3. When do bees fan the nectar?
   Ⓐ right after they find it
   Ⓑ right before they eat it
   Ⓒ right after they spread it
   Ⓓ right before they chew it

4. What is the last step in making honey?
   Ⓐ closing the comb
   Ⓑ finding the nectar
   Ⓒ fanning the comb
   Ⓓ carrying the nectar

STRATEGY PRACTICE   Write something you learned about how bees make honey.

_____

_____

Cause and Effect

Students practice the skill by looking for what happens (the effect) and why it happens (the cause).

Fact and Opinion

Students determine whether parts of the passage can be proved (facts) or represent what someone thinks or feels (opinions).

DAY 1

Introduce the *Cause and Effect* skill to students. Say: **If I drop a book on my toes, what will happen?** (It will hurt. I will have pain.) **Dropping the book is the cause of the pain. The pain is the effect of dropping the book. Good readers look for what happens—the effect—and why it happens—the cause.** Provide several additional examples, asking students to identify the *cause*s and the *effect*s. Review the *Visualization* strategy, which was taught during Week 2. Tell students that forming mental pictures of events in a story can help them understand causes and effects. Read the instructions at the top of the page aloud. Direct students to read the passage and to complete the activities. Review the answers to the skill practice activity together, pointing out the cause and the effect in items 2, 3, and 4. Then read the directions for the strategy practice activity aloud. Direct students to complete the activity. Allow time for students to share their responses.

DAY 2

Remind students of the skill, and review the *Organization* strategy, which was taught during Week 3. Then say: **As you read, notice how each paragraph tells about a different effect of the same cause, exercise.** Read the instructions at the top of the page aloud, and then have students read the passage. After they read, direct students to complete the skill and strategy practice activities. Discuss the reasons that should be underlined (makes muscles stronger; helps your bones; helps your brain grow).

DAY 3

Introduce the *Fact and Opinion* skill to students. Hold up a storybook and say: **If I say that this is the best story I have ever read, I am telling you my opinion. You might think that another story is better. If I say, "The title of this book is (book's title)," that is a fact. We can look at the cover and see the name. A fact is something you can prove to be true. If I say this is the best book in the room, that is an opinion. An opinion is what someone thinks.** Read the instructions at the top of the page aloud. After students have read the passage, complete the activities together, clarifying the difference between fact and opinion. Review the *Visualization* strategy if necessary. Allow students time to complete the strategy practice activity and to share their responses.

DAY 4

Remind students of the skill, and read the instructions at the top of the page aloud. After students have read the passage, complete the skill practice activity and review the answers together. Guide students through the strategy practice activity, which applies the *Organization* strategy. Point out that the writer organized the first three paragraphs by first stating an opinion, followed by facts. The final paragraph is completely opinion.

DAY 5

Tell students they will practice both the *Cause and Effect* and *Fact and Opinion* skills as they read about a pet store. Remind students of how the *Visualization* strategy can help them to have a clearer understanding of what they read. Then read the instructions at the top of the page aloud. After students have read the passage, complete the skill practice activity and review the answers together. Ask students to point out additional opinions in the passage not addressed in the activity items (parrot is clever; owner has a fun job; etc.). After students have completed the strategy practice activity, discuss their responses.

READ THE PASSAGE Look for reasons why things happen.

The Promise

"Remember, she likes to be petted on the head like this," Ben said to Sam. Ben petted Mousey's long, gray fur. Mousey purred. "Mousey is a very shy cat. But she likes you. Will you watch her while I am at my grandma's?"

"Sure," Sam said. She was happy to help. When Ben left, Sam took care of Mousey. She gave her food and water each day. She petted her. She let Mousey play with a pink and green ball.

One day, Maria called. She said, "We're going to the mountains for the weekend. We're staying in a red log cabin. I can bring a friend. We can play in the snow!" At first, Sam felt happy. Then she remembered Mousey.

"I can't go," Sam said sadly. "I have a promise to keep."

When Ben came home, he thanked Sam for taking care of Mousey. Sam felt proud.

SKILL PRACTICE Read the question. Fill in the bubble next to the correct answer.

1. Ben needs help with his _____.
   Ⓐ cat
   Ⓑ friend
   Ⓒ house
   Ⓓ grandma

2. Ben asks Sam to watch Mousey because Ben _____.
   Ⓐ is sick
   Ⓑ is going to his grandma's house
   Ⓒ does not like Mousey
   Ⓓ is going to the mountains

3. Sam kept her promise, so she _____.
   Ⓐ goes to play in the snow
   Ⓑ forgets about Mousey
   Ⓒ visits her grandmother
   Ⓓ does not go to the mountains

4. Why does Sam feel proud of herself?
   Ⓐ Mousey liked her.
   Ⓑ Ben thanked her.
   Ⓒ She took good care of Mousey.
   Ⓓ Maria invited her to the mountains.

STRATEGY PRACTICE Underline the sentences that helped you visualize what Mousey looks like and what she does.

Look for reasons why exercise is good for you.

Exercise

You probably have heard that exercise is good for your body. Do you know why? Here are some reasons.

Exercise makes muscles stronger. If you use your arm, leg, and back muscles, they will stay strong. The heart is a muscle, too. If it is strong, then it will pump more blood.

Exercise also helps your bones. If you run, hike, and dance, then your bones get stronger.

And did you know that exercise is good for your mind, too? Exercise helps your brain grow. Then you can learn and remember things better.

So what are you waiting for? Turn off the TV and let's go!

SKILL PRACTICE Read the question. Fill in the bubble next to the correct answer.

1. What is the passage about?
   - Ⓐ places to exercise
   - Ⓑ people who exercise
   - Ⓒ how exercise is good
   - Ⓓ how to exercise better

2. How does exercise help your bones?
   - Ⓐ It makes them whiter.
   - Ⓑ It makes them lighter
   - Ⓒ It makes them longer.
   - Ⓓ It makes them stronger.

3. When the heart is strong, it will _____.
   - Ⓐ be a muscle
   - Ⓑ remember better
   - Ⓒ pump more blood
   - Ⓓ hike and dance

4. Exercise helps your brain grow, and then you can _____.
   - Ⓐ learn
   - Ⓑ jump
   - Ⓒ swim
   - Ⓓ dance

STRATEGY PRACTICE Underline three ways that exercise helps your body.

READ THE PASSAGE   Look for facts and opinions about hummingbirds.

A Special Bird

See that bright flash of color in the garden? It's a hummingbird, the cutest of all birds! Its wings move so fast that they are a blur. The wings make a humming sound.

Hummingbirds are fun to watch when they fly. This tiny bird can fly very fast. It can fly to the left. It can fly to the right. It can even fly upside down! The hummingbird can also stay in one place. It floats above a flower. It uses its long beak to suck nectar from the flower. Then, in a flash, the hummingbird is gone!

Hummingbirds eat all day long, about once every ten minutes. Their hearts beat very, very fast. Hummingbirds are smart, too. They can remember where to find flowers from the year before.

Sometimes, hummingbirds take short rests. They like to stretch in the sun. They like to take baths in puddles. They like to sit on branches in the rain. They even play in sprinklers! These tiny birds are a special treat to see.

SKILL PRACTICE   Read the question. Fill in the bubble next to the correct answer.

1. The writer thinks hummingbirds are _____.

   Ⓐ cute

   Ⓑ boring

   Ⓒ slow

   Ⓓ silly

2. It is a fact that these birds _____.

   Ⓐ are a treat to see

   Ⓑ are the cutest birds

   Ⓒ make a humming sound

   Ⓓ are fun to watch

3. Which of these is an opinion?

   Ⓐ Hummingbirds have tiny hearts.

   Ⓑ Hummingbirds can fly upside down.

   Ⓒ Hummingbirds eat all day.

   Ⓓ Hummingbirds are fun to watch when they fly.

4. Which of these is an opinion?

   Ⓐ Hummingbirds fly fast.

   Ⓑ Hummingbirds are a treat to see.

   Ⓒ Hummingbirds have long beaks.

   Ⓓ Hummingbirds float above flowers.

STRATEGY PRACTICE   Underline words and phrases in the passage that helped you picture a hummingbird.

READ THE PASSAGE   Look for facts and opinions about the ballgame.

Take Me Out to the Ballgame

A baseball game is a lot of fun. People sit all around the field. They wear team colors. They wear hats like the players. They wave team flags.

The pitcher is the most interesting player to watch. He stands on a little hill of dirt. It's called the mound. He winds up and throws the ball really fast. Sometimes the batter has to jump out of the way.

It's exciting when a batter hits a home run. He runs and touches all the bases. Loud music plays and pictures flash on the scoreboard. People in the crowd clap and yell. "Our team is the best!" they shout.

The game gets boring if nobody hits the ball. Time passes slowly. But get a tasty hot dog, and you'll be glad you came.

SKILL PRACTICE   Read the question. Fill in the bubble next to the correct answer.

1. Which one is the writer's opinion?

   Ⓐ Pitchers throw the ball fast.

   Ⓑ Baseball games are fun.

   Ⓒ There are hot dogs to eat.

   Ⓓ People wear team colors.

2. Which of these is a fact?

   Ⓐ The game can be boring.

   Ⓑ You will be glad you came.

   Ⓒ A home run is exciting.

   Ⓓ The pitcher stands on the mound.

3. Which of these is a fact?

   Ⓐ The pitcher throws a ball.

   Ⓑ Time passes slowly.

   Ⓒ It is boring if there are no hits.

   Ⓓ Our team is the best.

4. Which one is an opinion?

   Ⓐ The crowd yells.

   Ⓑ The batter touches the bases.

   Ⓒ The pitcher is interesting.

   Ⓓ The people wear hats.

STRATEGY PRACTICE   Find and underline one opinion in each paragraph.

READ THE PASSAGE Notice what the writer thinks about the different animals.

Pet Store

It's fun to visit a pet store. There are different animals to see.

The big parrot is very colorful. It is clever, too. "Hello!" it says to people who walk by.

The kittens are soft and cute. People love to hold them. The kittens sleep a lot. Then they wake up and meow. They need food and fresh water every day.

There are many different kinds of lizards. One of them is the baby water dragon. It is very pretty. It has green, scaly skin and gold eyes. Bumps on its back make it look like a little dragon. It lives inside a glass box. It has a little tub of water to swim in. There are branches in the box, too. Water dragons have long claws on their feet to help them climb. They like to eat bugs, too.

The pet store owner is busy. He has a fun job. He takes good care of the animals and tells people what the animals need.

SKILL PRACTICE Read the question. Fill in the bubble next to the correct answer.

1. **Which of these is an opinion?**
   - Ⓐ Kittens meow.
   - Ⓑ Kittens need food.
   - Ⓒ Water dragons climb.
   - Ⓓ Water dragons are pretty.

2. **It is a fact that some parrots _____.**
   - Ⓐ can talk
   - Ⓑ meow
   - Ⓒ have scaly skin
   - Ⓓ swim in a tub of water

3. **Based on the passage, people like to hold kittens because they _____.**
   - Ⓐ sleep a lot
   - Ⓑ are soft and cute
   - Ⓒ meow when they are awake
   - Ⓓ say hello when people go by

4. **Why is the pet store owner busy?**
   - Ⓐ He likes his job.
   - Ⓑ He sleeps a lot.
   - Ⓒ He must talk to the parrot.
   - Ⓓ He has many animals to care for.

STRATEGY PRACTICE Underline words in the passage that helped you picture what a water dragon looks like.

Compare and Contrast

Students look for similarities and differences between two or more people or things.

Make Inferences

Students look for clues in the passage and draw upon their own experience to understand information that is not directly stated.

DAY 1

To introduce the *Compare and Contrast* skill to students, show an apple and an orange. Ask: **How are the two the same?** (Both are fruits. Both are round. Both taste sweet. Both have seeds.). Then ask: **How are the two different?** (different colors; smooth skin, bumpy skin; apple has seeds in center, orange has seeds throughout; etc.). Say: **We have just compared and contrasted an apple and an orange. We have looked at ways they are the same and different.** Read the instructions at the top of the page aloud. Then remind students of the *Ask Questions* strategy, which was taught during Week 5. Say: **We will stop after each paragraph and ask questions about what we read.** Then read the passage together, stopping after each paragraph to think of and list questions that can be answered by the passage. Direct students to complete the skill practice activity, and then review the answers together, pointing out that items 1, 2, and 3 are compare and contrast items. For the strategy practice activity, review the list of questions posed during the reading of the passage and mark those that were answered. Allow students to choose a question to complete the item.

DAY 2

Remind students of the skill, and read the instructions at the top of the page aloud. Then remind students of the *Monitor Comprehension* strategy, which was taught during Week 6. Say: **You will need to pay attention to how well you understand the information in the passage.** Read the passage together. Stop after each paragraph and ask if the information given told how the sisters are alike or how they are different (1—alike; 2 & 3—different; 4—alike). Complete the skill practice activity and review the answers together. Then read the directions for the strategy practice activity aloud and remind students that because they monitored their comprehension as they read the passage, they will remember other ways to compare the sisters. Work as a group to write choices for the strategy practice activity, helping students to find information not used in the skill practice activity items.

DAY 3

Introduce the *Make Inferences* skill to students. Say: **Good readers are like detectives. They look for clues in a passage that help them figure out things. For example, if I read that a character's teeth were chattering and he was shivering and he was outside in the snow, I would know he was cold. The author would not have to write that. I could make that inference.** Read the instructions at the top of the page aloud. Then remind students of the *Ask Questions* strategy. Say: **As you read, stop and ask yourself questions about what you read to make sure you understand it.** After students have read the passage, complete the skill practice activity together. Help students understand that the answers to the items were not directly stated in the story and that they needed to use clues and make inferences to find the answers. Direct students to complete the strategy practice activity, and allow individuals to share their questions.

DAY 4

Remind students of the skill, and read the instructions at the top of the page aloud. Call students' attention to the fact that they will be practicing the *Monitor Comprehension* strategy. After students have read the passage, complete the activities and review the answers together.

DAY 5

Tell students they will practice both the *Compare and Contrast* and *Make Inferences* skills. Read the instructions at the top of the page aloud. Say: **You will read about a family that is deciding where they will take a vacation.** Remind students of the *Ask Questions* strategy. Have students brainstorm questions they would have about vacation places. Record the questions on the board, and direct students to write a question in the space provided for the strategy practice activity. Have students read the passage, and then invite volunteers to share their questions and discuss how it helped them set a purpose for reading. Then direct students to complete the skill practice activity. Review the answers together.

Daily Reading Comprehension • EMC 3452 • © Evan-Moor Corp.

READ THE PASSAGE   Think of questions you have about the information.

Backyard Birds

Some people like to see birds in their yards. They like the pretty colors. They like to hear birds sing. People put bird feeders in their yards to get birds to visit.

Some feeders hold seeds. Most birds eat seeds. Pigeons and doves like corn, too. Woodpeckers and blue jays like cakes of hard fat. Many birds also like popcorn and bread. But watch out! The squirrels like these foods, too.

Feeders for hummingbirds hold sugar water. Some people color it red. The hummingbirds remember where the feeders are. They come back again and again.

People who do not have yards can hang bird feeders near their windows. The birds will come to eat the food. "Thank you!" they will tweet through the glass.

SKILL PRACTICE   Read the question. Fill in the bubble next to the correct answer.

1. Birds and squirrels both like _____.

    Ⓐ cake

    Ⓑ bread

    Ⓒ hard fat

    Ⓓ sugar water

2. Pigeons and doves both like _____.

    Ⓐ corn

    Ⓑ hard fat

    Ⓒ sugar water

    Ⓓ bread

3. Which bird is different from the others because it drinks its food?

    Ⓐ dove

    Ⓑ pigeon

    Ⓒ woodpecker

    Ⓓ hummingbird

4. Which food would bring the most kinds of birds to a feeder?

    Ⓐ fat

    Ⓑ bread

    Ⓒ seeds

    Ⓓ sugar water

STRATEGY PRACTICE   Write a question you had that the passage answered.

_____

READ THE PASSAGE Think about how Rani and Dara are alike and different.

Two Sisters

Rani and Dara are sisters. They are alike in some ways. The two girls have the same parents. They live in the same house. They even share the same bedroom. Rani and Dara walk to school together each morning. They do their homework at the same table. Both girls like music, and both like to ride bikes. They go on long rides together.

Rani and Dara are different in some ways, too. Rani is tall. Her hair and eyes are brown. Dara is short. Her hair is blond, and her eyes are blue. Both girls have nice smiles, but their smiles are not the same shape.

Rani loves to paint. She is very good at math. Dara loves to swim. She is a good soccer player. When Rani grows up, she wants to be a teacher. Dara wants to be a swim coach.

Both girls are hard workers. Both can reach their goals.

SKILL PRACTICE Read the question. Fill in the bubble next to the correct answer.

1. Both sisters _____.
   Ⓐ have dark hair
   Ⓑ have blue eyes
   Ⓒ like to ride bikes
   Ⓓ like to play soccer

2. Each girl has a different _____.
   Ⓐ family
   Ⓑ goal
   Ⓒ house
   Ⓓ bedroom

3. Which one is true about both girls?
   Ⓐ They are hard workers.
   Ⓑ They both love to paint.
   Ⓒ They both love to swim.
   Ⓓ Their smiles are the same.

4. The sisters are different because _____.
   Ⓐ Dara paints, but Rani swims
   Ⓑ Rani is tall, but Dara is short
   Ⓒ Dara is good at math, but Rani is a good soccer player
   Ⓓ Rani is blond, but Dara's hair is dark

STRATEGY PRACTICE Write a sentence that compares or contrasts the sisters.

_____

READ THE PASSAGE Think about what a guide dog probably does on a usual day.

Guide Dogs

Guide dogs help people who cannot see. They help blind people go places. They help them do things they could not do alone.

When a guide dog walking on the sidewalk reaches a curb, it stops. The dog stops until it knows it is safe. Then the dog crosses the street with its person. The dog does not walk too fast. It stays near the person it guides.

Guide dogs see things for blind people. They lead blind people around poles. They lead them around branches hanging over paths. They keep blind people from tripping over cracks in the sidewalk. Guide dogs help blind people walk through crowded stores. They lead them onto buses. When the person sits, the dog lies down. The dog does not chase cats that go by.

A guide dog learns more every day about what its person needs. The two form a very close team. They go through life together.

SKILL PRACTICE Read the question. Fill in the bubble next to the correct answer.

1. Guide dogs are probably very _____.

   Ⓐ lazy

   Ⓑ smart

   Ⓒ funny

   Ⓓ scared

2. A guide dog's main job is most likely to _____.

   Ⓐ ride in buses

   Ⓑ shop in stores

   Ⓒ keep a person safe

   Ⓓ find people who are lost

3. Guide dogs are most likely good at _____.

   Ⓐ finding food

   Ⓑ chasing cats

   Ⓒ running wildly

   Ⓓ waiting quietly

4. Guide dogs and their people probably _____.

   Ⓐ care about each other

   Ⓑ have the same friends

   Ⓒ live in separate places

   Ⓓ eat the same kind of food

STRATEGY PRACTICE What is a question you would ask the owner of a guide dog?

_____

_____

READ THE PASSAGE Stop as you read and ask yourself what is happening.

Field Trip

Ms. Terra's class was going on a field trip. The children were happy. A big yellow bus was waiting in front of the school. It took them to the aquarium. An aquarium is where fish and other sea creatures live.

At the aquarium, the children and Ms. Terra were greeted by a young man named Carlo. Carlo led them into a big room. One wall of the room was made of glass. Behind the glass, fish were swimming through the seawater.

The fish were different sizes and colors. Some were round. Others were flat with stripes. Long, thin eels that looked like snakes curled through plants at the bottom. Carlo told the children where the fish came from and what they eat.

Next, Carlo took the class to the tide pool area. It had big rocks and sand with pools of saltwater. They saw crabs and a spiky sea urchin. Everyone touched a sea star. The class ate lunch outside before going back to their school.

SKILL PRACTICE Read the question. Fill in the bubble next to the correct answer.

1. You can tell that Carlo _____.
   - Ⓐ is new at the aquarium
   - Ⓑ has met the class before
   - Ⓒ knows a lot about sea life
   - Ⓓ wants to eat with the class

2. All animals in this aquarium probably _____.
   - Ⓐ look the same
   - Ⓑ are not safe to touch
   - Ⓒ look like snakes
   - Ⓓ live in saltwater

3. What is likely true about the tide pool?
   - Ⓐ There is no water in it.
   - Ⓑ Animals live there.
   - Ⓒ You can eat lunch in it.
   - Ⓓ People can swim in it.

4. Which one is most likely true about the field trip?
   - Ⓐ The class learned about sea animals.
   - Ⓑ Ms. Terra left early.
   - Ⓒ Carlo drove the bus.
   - Ⓓ The fish were scared.

STRATEGY PRACTICE Write two things you learned about the aquarium.

_____

_____

READ THE PASSAGE Try to remember the things the family can do at each place.

A Hard Choice

Summer is almost here. The Satos are planning a trip. They like the beach. They like the lake. Which place should they go to? Both places are warm. Both places are pretty. Both have many things to do.

If the family goes to the beach, they can play in the waves. They can play in the soft sand. They can fly a kite. They can walk on the pier and buy taffy. They can feed bits of bread to the sea gulls.

If the family goes to the lake, they can camp in a tent. They can row a boat and catch fish. They can cook the fish for dinner. They can sit under the stars beside a campfire. Squirrels with fluffy tails will chatter in the pine trees. The jays will screech overhead as the family hikes in the woods.

It is hard to choose between the two places because both are very nice.

SKILL PRACTICE Read the question. Fill in the bubble next to the correct answer.

1. Both places have _____.
   Ⓐ gulls
   Ⓑ water
   Ⓒ soft sand
   Ⓓ taffy

2. Only the beach has _____.
   Ⓐ boats to row in
   Ⓑ tents to camp in
   Ⓒ waves to play in
   Ⓓ woods to hike in

3. The Satos probably like to _____.
   Ⓐ feed fish
   Ⓑ build boats
   Ⓒ make candy
   Ⓓ play outside

4. The Satos most likely want to _____.
   Ⓐ have a fun trip
   Ⓑ play in the snow
   Ⓒ learn about stars
   Ⓓ buy a new house

STRATEGY PRACTICE Write a question you had and the answer you found in the passage.

_____

Character and Setting

Students study a passage to better understand who or what is at the center of the action and when and where the action takes place.

Fantasy and Reality

Students identify which things in the passage could or could not happen in real life.

DAY 1

Introduce the *Character and Setting* skill to students. Show an illustration from a book that includes people, animals, and an easily identifiable setting. Ask: **What people and animals are in this story? These are the characters. What kind of place do you see? This is the setting of the story.** Reinforce the terms by naming some familiar stories and asking students to tell the characters and the settings. Read the instructions at the top of the page aloud. Then remind students of the *Make Connections* strategy, which was taught during Week 1. Say: **To better understand what they read, good readers think about how a passage relates to things they know or have done. They make connections with the text.** After students have read the passage, make a list of the characters, and discuss the setting. Direct students to complete the skill practice activity, and then review the answers together. After students have completed the strategy practice activity, allow volunteers to share their responses.

DAY 2

Remind students of the skill, and review what a *character* is and what a *setting* is. Then read the instructions at the top of the page aloud. Remind students of the *Visualization* strategy, which was taught during Week 2. Say: **As you read, visualize the characters and the setting in your mind.** After students have read the passage, brainstorm words and phrases that would describe the characters (Rita—quick-thinking, sure of herself, helpful; Skateboarder—careless, unsafe, injured; Rita's brothers—thought Rita was a baby, proud of Rita at the end). Complete the activities and review the answers together. Allow time for students to share what they underlined in response to the strategy practice activity prompt.

DAY 3

Introduce the *Fantasy and Reality* skill to students. Make two lists on the board, one with fantasy items (cow jumped over the moon, fairy princess, talking donkey, etc.); the other with real items (2nd-grade student, a dog that barks, a car with a driver, etc.). Then read each list aloud and ask students how they would describe the things (make-believe or real). Say: **Another word for make-believe is *fantasy*. What is real is called *reality*.** Read the instructions at the top of the page aloud. Remind students of the *Make Connections* strategy. Say: **Making connections is a good way to tell if something is real or make-believe because you can compare what you are reading to your own experiences.** Then have students read the passage. When students have finished, complete the skill practice activity and review the answers together. Direct students to reread the passage in order to complete the strategy practice activity. Allow time for volunteers to share their responses.

DAY 4

Remind students of the *Fantasy and Reality* skill, and read the instructions at the top of the page aloud. Remind students of the *Visualization* strategy and tell them to make a mental picture of what they read. After students have read the passage, complete the skill practice activity and review the answers together. Then read the strategy practice activity instructions aloud. Say: **There were words in the passage that told how something looked, sounded, felt, smelled, or tasted. These words helped you visualize what was happening.** Complete the strategy practice activity together.

DAY 5

Tell students they will practice both the *Character and Setting* and *Fantasy and Reality* skills. Remind students to make connections with the text to learn about the characters and to decide what could and could not happen. Then read the instructions at the top of the page aloud. Direct students to read the passage and to complete the skill practice activity. Review the answers together. Then direct students to complete the strategy practice activity, and allow time for sharing responses.

Daily Reading Comprehension • EMC 3452 • © Evan-Moor Corp.

READ THE PASSAGE   Pay attention to where the characters are and what they do.

Train Ride

My big brother's wife had a baby boy! His name is Jack, and he lives far away. We are taking a train to see him. We will meet the baby tomorrow. My sister and I can't wait!

We had to stand far away from the track when the train came into the station. It was very loud. We found our car and climbed aboard. A man came by and took our tickets.

The train cars have big seats. My sister sits and reads. I enjoy looking out the windows. We pass green fields. We pass houses and stores.

One of the cars of the train is for eating. It has tables in it. We order food, just like in a restaurant. I get fried chicken. My sister gets a hamburger.

We'll sleep on the train tonight. My sister and I have a little room of our own. Two beds like bunk beds fold down from the walls. Mine feels nice! The train wheels go "clackety-clack."

"Clackety-clack, Baby Jack," I think as I go to sleep.

SKILL PRACTICE   Read the question. Fill in the bubble next to the correct answer.

1. The person telling the story _____.

    Ⓐ eats a hamburger on the train

    Ⓑ is riding alone

    Ⓒ cannot go to sleep

    Ⓓ likes to ride on the train

2. When the characters are ready to sleep, they go to _____.

    Ⓐ the car for eating

    Ⓑ the back of the train

    Ⓒ the train station

    Ⓓ a car with bunk beds

3. The person telling the story wants to _____.

    Ⓐ eat at a table

    Ⓑ see the baby

    Ⓒ stay at the station

    Ⓓ keep the train ticket

4. The train station _____.

    Ⓐ is loud when the train comes

    Ⓑ is a place to sit and read

    Ⓒ has big seats

    Ⓓ has two beds

STRATEGY PRACTICE   Underline a part of the story that you would like to do.

READ THE PASSAGE Think about how you would describe the characters.

The Youngest One

Rita was the youngest in her family. She had two big brothers. They treated her like a baby. They would not take her places with them. "You are too young," they said. "You should stay home."

"I am old enough!" Rita said. But they did not listen.

One day, Rita was playing outside on the swings. A boy with no helmet rode by on a skateboard. He hit a bump. The skateboard stopped, but the boy kept going! He landed on his head. The boy sat up and held his head. He was hurt. Rita leaped from the swing. "I will get help," she told the boy.

Rita ran into the house. She grabbed the phone and dialed 9-1-1. She told the person who answered what she had seen. Down the street came an ambulance! It took the boy to the hospital.

"Rita, you did well!" her brothers said.

SKILL PRACTICE Read the question. Fill in the bubble next to the correct answer.

1. **What makes Rita upset?**

   Ⓐ Her mother will not take her to town.

   Ⓑ Her brothers treat her like a baby.

   Ⓒ She cannot go outside to play.

   Ⓓ She cannot use the phone.

2. **Rita shows that she can _____.**

   Ⓐ get help

   Ⓑ ride in an ambulance

   Ⓒ help the doctor

   Ⓓ ride a skateboard

3. **Where does the boy get hurt?**

   Ⓐ at the hospital

   Ⓑ in Rita's house

   Ⓒ on a street near a store

   Ⓓ in front of Rita's house

4. **The boy on the skateboard _____.**

   Ⓐ is friends with Rita

   Ⓑ is a safe skateboarder

   Ⓒ should have been wearing a helmet

   Ⓓ asked Rita to call 9-1-1

STRATEGY PRACTICE Underline a part of the story that made a big picture in your mind.

READ THE PASSAGE Look for things that are make-believe.

The Magic Fish

A poor fisherman lived with his wife in a shack by the sea. His wife was not happy. "Why can't I have pretty clothes and beautiful jewels?" the wife whined.

One day, the fisherman felt a tug on his fishing line. He pulled in a shiny, silver fish. Imagine his surprise when the fish spoke!

"Let me go and I will grant a wish," begged the fish.

The excited fisherman raced home. He told his wife about the fish.

"I wish for a big house. I want fine clothes and fancy food!" cried the wife. Right then, the wish came true.

Before long, the wife became unhappy again. She wanted more riches.

"Go find the fish. Tell him I want all the gold in the world," the wife ordered.

The poor fisherman did as his wife told him. He sat near the sea. He called for the fish. The fish listened as the man told his wife's wish.

"She asks for too much!" shouted the fish. "You will find your wife in your little shack once more." The fish dove into the sea and was never seen again.

SKILL PRACTICE Read the question. Fill in the bubble next to the correct answer.

1. **Which of these is make-believe?**
   Ⓐ a fish that talks
   Ⓑ a man catching a fish
   Ⓒ a wife who is unhappy
   Ⓓ a fish diving into the sea

2. **Which of these is real?**
   Ⓐ a fish shouting
   Ⓑ a fish listening to a man
   Ⓒ a fish tugging on a fisherman's line
   Ⓓ a fish making a wish come true

3. **Which of these does the passage tell you?**
   Ⓐ Do not make wishes.
   Ⓑ Do not be greedy.
   Ⓒ Do not catch fish.
   Ⓓ Do not be unhappy.

4. **Which one might the magic fish say?**
   Ⓐ "It is wrong to change your mind."
   Ⓑ "You should never ask for gold."
   Ⓒ "Be happy with what you are given."
   Ⓓ "It is wrong to ask for help."

STRATEGY PRACTICE Complete the sentence.

I would ask a magic fish to _____.

READ THE PASSAGE Think about what could and could <u>not</u> happen.

Helpful Hilda

Mrs. Song sat at the blue kitchen table. She was waiting for Hilda. Soon, a shiny metal robot rolled noisily into the kitchen.

"Good morning, Mrs. Song," the robot beeped.

"Good morning, Hilda," Mrs. Song said. "Are Jin and Mr. Song awake yet?"

"Yes, Mrs. Song," Hilda beeped. "I will make their breakfast now." Hilda rolled around the kitchen, beeping and clicking. The robot found a black frying pan. Then it found some eggs and yellow cheese. Soon, Hilda was busy making breakfast.

Mr. Song and Jin walked into the kitchen. Mrs. Song smiled at them.

"Good morning, Mom," Jin said. "That food smells great, Hilda."

"Hurry up and eat," Mrs. Song said. "My shuttle to Jupiter is coming soon, so Hilda will fly you to school today."

SKILL PRACTICE Read the question. Fill in the bubble next to the correct answer.

1. **Which of these could be real?**
   Ⓐ A robot makes breakfast.
   Ⓑ A woman has a robot that can think.
   Ⓒ A boy eats breakfast before school.
   Ⓓ A robot takes a boy to school.

2. **Who in the passage <u>cannot</u> be real?**
   Ⓐ a woman named Mrs. Song
   Ⓑ a flying robot named Hilda
   Ⓒ a boy named Jin Song
   Ⓓ a man named Mr. Song

3. **What does Mrs. Song do that <u>cannot</u> be real?**
   Ⓐ She tells Jin to eat breakfast.
   Ⓑ She takes a trip to Jupiter.
   Ⓒ She sits at a kitchen table.
   Ⓓ She smiles at Mr. Song.

4. **What does Jin do that <u>cannot</u> be real?**
   Ⓐ He wakes up.
   Ⓑ He eats breakfast.
   Ⓒ He talks to his parents.
   Ⓓ He flies to school.

STRATEGY PRACTICE Circle the words in the passage that describe how something looks or sounds.

Name: _____

READ THE PASSAGE What experiences in the passage could and could <u>not</u> happen?

Move to Mars

"I don't want to move to Mars!" my sister cried. "My friends are *here*."

"I think you will like it there," said Mom. "You will have your own rocket."

"Cool!" my little brother said. "Vroom-Vroom!" He ran through the house.

Our father is a builder. His job would be on Mars. I did not know if I would like it there.

The trip to Mars took a long time. When we got there, we stretched our legs. The ground was covered with red dust. Our new house was shaped like a big cake. My bed was different from the one on Earth. It floated around the room! We had a robot dog named Tin Can. He was made of metal!

The children at school were nice. Some of them looked like us. Others had blue faces and pointed ears. We made new friends and had fun with our rockets. Even my sister liked life on Mars more than she thought she would.

SKILL PRACTICE Read the question. Fill in the bubble next to the correct answer.

1. **The little brother is eager to _____.**
   Ⓐ have a pet
   Ⓑ have a rocket
   Ⓒ go to a new school
   Ⓓ go away from Mars

2. **How does the person who tells the story feel about moving to Mars?**
   Ⓐ She really wants to go there.
   Ⓑ She thinks it will be fun.
   Ⓒ She does not like it on Earth.
   Ⓓ She is not sure if she will like Mars.

3. **Which one is make-believe?**
   Ⓐ children who have blue faces
   Ⓑ people who move to new places
   Ⓒ brothers who run around the house
   Ⓓ sisters who want to be with friends

4. **Which one is real?**
   Ⓐ metal dogs
   Ⓑ beds that float
   Ⓒ new school friends
   Ⓓ family trips to Mars

STRATEGY PRACTICE Write about something in the passage that you would like to do.

_____

_____

Author's Purpose

Students think about why an author wrote a particular passage.

Prediction

Students use clues from the text and their own background knowledge to anticipate what is likely to happen next or what information will come next.

DAY 1

Introduce the *Author's Purpose* skill to students. Say: **Think about things you have written. You had a reason for writing it. Common purposes for writing are to tell a story that entertains, to tell how to do something, to give information about something, and to persuade someone to think or do a certain thing. The reason for writing is called** *Author's Purpose.* Give several examples of common types of writing, and help students determine the author's purpose (e.g., A nonfiction story tells us more about a topic. A recipe tells us how to make something. A Dr. Seuss story entertains.). Read the instructions at the top of the page aloud. Then read the first paragraph aloud to students. Remind students of the *Ask Questions* strategy, which was taught during Week 5. Model questions students can ask themselves as they read to help them determine the author's purpose (e.g., *Why did the author write this? What does the author want to tell me?* etc.). Have students write their question in the space provided for the strategy practice activity. After students have read the passage, complete the skill practice activity together. Read all of the answer choices for each item, and let students decide on the correct answers with a partner. Discuss students' choices and, as a group, determine the author's purpose. Then direct students to complete the strategy practice activity. Allow students to share their responses.

DAY 2

Remind students of the *Author's Purpose* skill and the common reasons why authors write (to entertain, to teach, to inform/tell, to persuade). Read the instructions at the top of the page aloud. Remind students of the *Make Connections* strategy, which was taught during Week 1. Say: **Use the** *Make Connections* **strategy to help you understand how the class will decorate their room.** Direct students to read the passage and to complete the activities. Then review the answers together. Allow students to share their responses to the strategy practice activity.

DAY 3

Introduce the *Prediction* skill to students. Say: **When we predict, we use clues from the text and our own experiences to figure out what will likely happen next.** Read the instructions at the top of the page aloud. Then remind students of the *Ask Questions* strategy. Tell students that as they read, they should ask themselves questions about what the children are doing. Then direct students to read the passage and to complete the skill practice activity. Review the answers together, asking students to tell which parts of the text verify their answers. Direct students to complete the strategy practice activity, and then pair students or share student questions as a group.

DAY 4

Remind students of the *Prediction* skill. Then read items 1, 2, and 3 of the skill practice activity aloud. Point out the signal word *probably.* Say: **When we see this word in a question, we are likely going to practice making inferences or predicting.** Read the instructions at the top of the page aloud. Then remind students of the *Make Connections* strategy. Say: **It's easier to predict if we make connections between the text and our own experiences.** Direct students to read the passage and to complete the skill practice activity. Review the answers together. For the strategy practice activity, pair students or complete it as a group.

DAY 5

Tell students they will practice both the *Author's Purpose* and *Prediction* skills. Read the instructions at the top of the page aloud. Then remind students of the *Ask Questions* strategy. Say: **As you read, ask questions about what you think might happen next or why the author wrote this passage.** Direct students to read the passage and to complete the skill and strategy practice activities. Review the answers together.

READ THE PASSAGE Think about why the author wrote the passage.

Breakfast for You

What did you have for breakfast today? You might have had a bowl of cereal with milk and a banana. Your parents bought these foods at the store. But how did the food get to the store?

A farmer in a warm place grew the bananas. The farmer sent the bananas to where you live. They came on a boat or an airplane.

Your cereal might be made from wheat. Wheat is grown on big farms in the middle part of the USA. The farmer cut the wheat. Then he sold it to the people who made the cereal.

You know that milk comes from cows. Cows are raised in places with lots of good green grass. The cows eat the grass. Then they make healthful milk for you to drink.

Lots of people in lots of places work to bring breakfast to your table.

SKILL PRACTICE Read the question. Fill in the bubble next to the correct answer.

1. The writer wants people to _____.
   - Ⓐ become farmers
   - Ⓑ go to the store for food
   - Ⓒ know where food comes from
   - Ⓓ drink lots of milk

2. The writer tells about wheat because _____.
   - Ⓐ your cereal might be made from it
   - Ⓑ it grows in the USA
   - Ⓒ it goes well with bananas
   - Ⓓ it is eaten by cows

3. The writer wants us to know that _____.
   - Ⓐ cows eat green grass
   - Ⓑ bananas go to stores in boats
   - Ⓒ farmers sell wheat
   - Ⓓ many people work to bring us food

4. What did you learn about breakfast foods?
   - Ⓐ Everyone eats the same kind of cereal.
   - Ⓑ They come from different places.
   - Ⓒ They all come from cows.
   - Ⓓ All of them are healthful.

STRATEGY PRACTICE What question did you ask before you read?

_____

_____

READ THE PASSAGE   Ask yourself why the author wrote the passage.

Class Vote

Friday was Parent Night. All the classrooms would be open. People would sell cookies in the hall. The students in Mr. Ray's class would show their room to their parents. The students wanted the room to look good. They were going to paint a big mural for the classroom wall.

What should they paint? Some wanted to paint white snow falling on houses. They wanted to paint children skating on a pond and building a big snowman. Some students wanted a picture of the sea. They wanted to paint bright yellow fish in blue water. They wanted to paint shiny gray dolphins jumping out of the water.

Mr. Ray held a vote. "Raise your hand if you want a picture with snow," he said. Half of the students raised their hands. "Raise your hand if you want a picture of the sea," he said. The other half of the students raised their hands. "It's a tie!" said Mr. Ray. The class painted murals with both pictures. Their parents liked them both.

SKILL PRACTICE   Read the question. Fill in the bubble next to the correct answer.

1. The author wrote the passage to _____.
   Ⓐ explain all about Parent Night
   Ⓑ tell how to decide something fairly
   Ⓒ make kids want to paint murals
   Ⓓ explain how to paint murals

2. Why does the author describe things the students want to paint?
   Ⓐ to show that the teacher is a good artist
   Ⓑ to show that the parents should decide
   Ⓒ to show that the mural ideas are not good
   Ⓓ to show that the students do not always agree on one idea

3. Why does the author describe the ideas for the murals?
   Ⓐ to help the reader picture them
   Ⓑ to explain what a mural is
   Ⓒ to show why people like murals
   Ⓓ to help students pick a mural

4. Why do you think the vote is a tie?
   Ⓐ to make the parents happy
   Ⓑ to make the class vote again
   Ⓒ to show that everyone can win
   Ⓓ to show that the teacher does not care

STRATEGY PRACTICE   Which mural would you have voted for? Why?

_____

_____

Name: _____

READ THE PASSAGE Look for clues that can help you predict what Nicky and Lena will likely do in the future.

Lemonade Stand

"I want to buy a skateboard," said Nicky. "But I do not have enough money. My dad said that if I pay for part of it, he will pay for the rest. How can I make some money?"

"I know!" said Lena. "You can sell lemonade. I'll help. We can sell it on the bike path. People who ride by will be thirsty."

The children found a folding table. It was in Lena's garage. Her mother helped them make lemonade. She baked some cookies, too. Nicky's father carried the table to the bike path. He sat on a bench and read a newspaper.

Nicky and Lena sat behind the table. A big sign said, "Lemonade and Cookies, 50 cents each." People saw the children sitting there. They also saw the sign. They stopped. Nicky and Lena were very busy!

Soon, all the lemonade was gone. The children smiled at each other.

SKILL PRACTICE Read the question. Fill in the bubble next to the correct answer.

1. What will the children probably do next?
   Ⓐ put the table away
   Ⓑ clean out a garage
   Ⓒ read the newspaper
   Ⓓ learn to bake cookies

2. Which of these might the children sell in the winter?
   Ⓐ ice cream
   Ⓑ juice pops
   Ⓒ hot chocolate
   Ⓓ cotton candy

3. What will Nicky likely buy with the money he makes?
   Ⓐ shoes
   Ⓑ a bike
   Ⓒ cookies
   Ⓓ a skateboard

4. Why do you think the children smile at the end of the passage?
   Ⓐ It is time to go home.
   Ⓑ They had sold a lot of lemonade.
   Ⓒ Nicky's father tells a joke.
   Ⓓ They are not busy.

STRATEGY PRACTICE Write a question you would ask the children about their lemonade stand.

_____

READ THE PASSAGE Ask yourself what the children will do next.

Snowed In

"I wish we could stay for one more day," I thought as I fell asleep. Winter camp had been such fun. Tomorrow we would leave the mountains and go home to the city.

It had snowed all day. Then it snowed all night. When I woke up, the whole world seemed to be covered in white. "There is too much snow on the road," our camp leader, Ms. Joy, said. "The bus is stuck. We will stay at camp for one more night. The roads will be clear by tomorrow."

"Hooray!" we shouted. We ran out the door. The snow was deep and soft. We dove into it with our arms open wide. We threw handfuls of it into the air. We threw balls of it at each other. We built a snow giant. As we played, the sun came out. It started melting some of the snow.

That night, we ate warm soup by the fire. We stayed up late and told stories. All the days at camp had been fun, but this last one was the best!

SKILL PRACTICE Read the question. Fill in the bubble next to the correct answer.

1. What will the children probably do right after they tell stories?

Ⓐ go to sleep

Ⓑ make soup

Ⓒ build a snow giant

Ⓓ leave the mountains

2. What will the leader probably say in the morning?

Ⓐ "The road is open."

Ⓑ "The snow is gone."

Ⓒ "We must stay all winter."

Ⓓ "We must clear the road."

3. Where will the children likely go next?

Ⓐ to a new camp

Ⓑ back to the city

Ⓒ into a snow cave

Ⓓ higher up in the mountains

4. How do you think the person telling the story feels about winter camp?

Ⓐ She wishes she had stayed home.

Ⓑ She had a really good time.

Ⓒ She wants to write a story about it.

Ⓓ She wanted to go home sooner.

STRATEGY PRACTICE Tell a partner about a time when you could <u>not</u> do what you had planned to do and what happened.

Daily Reading Comprehension • EMC 3452 • © Evan-Moor Corp.

READ THE PASSAGE   Ask yourself why the author wrote the passage.

Silly Squirrels

Summer was over. The air was getting colder. Leaves were falling from the trees. The squirrel family was gathering seeds and nuts. They would save them for later. They knew that food would be hard to find under the snow.

"I can jump higher than you can," one brother said.

"No you can't. Watch me," the other squirrel brother said.

"Who can find more acorns?" asked their mother. This put the brothers to work. Up and down the tree they went.

Then, there it was, at the end of a branch—the biggest acorn ever.

"I saw it first!" said one brother.

"No, I did," said the other. "It's mine!"

They both held on to the acorn. Neither one would let go. Then the acorn slipped. It fell to the ground and landed near a boy's feet.

"Hey, look at this big acorn," the boy said. And he put it in his pocket.

SKILL PRACTICE   Read the question. Fill in the bubble next to the correct answer.

1. The writer most likely wrote the passage to _____.

   Ⓐ teach a lesson

   Ⓑ show how leaves fall

   Ⓒ tell what squirrels eat

   Ⓓ show how big acorns are

2. What will the brothers probably do next time?

   Ⓐ yell at each other

   Ⓑ hold on to the acorn

   Ⓒ throw the acorn down

   Ⓓ share with each other

3. Which of these do you think the author would say?

   Ⓐ "If you find something, it is yours."

   Ⓑ "Sharing something is better than having nothing."

   Ⓒ "If you lose something, it is your fault."

   Ⓓ "Parents always know what is best."

4. The boy will most likely _____.

   Ⓐ put the acorn down

   Ⓑ give the acorn back

   Ⓒ take the acorn home

   Ⓓ look for a bigger acorn

STRATEGY PRACTICE   What question would you ask the author about the passage?

_____

Nonfiction Text Features
Students look at text features, such as headings and captions, to better understand what they read.

Visual Information
Students discover how pictures, charts, graphs, and other visual elements can explain more about a topic.

DAY 1

Explain to students that nonfiction text features are related to the main body of the text but different from it and include features such as a table of contents, glossary, captions, headings, bold vocabulary words, etc. Say: **We often find these special features in nonfiction books. It is important to pay attention to nonfiction text features because they help us understand what we are reading.** Remind students of the *Determine Important Information* strategy, which was taught during Week 4. Then explain to students that looking for nonfiction text features can help them identify which information is most important. Read the instructions at the top of the page aloud. Tell students that a glossary is an example of a nonfiction text feature. Read the glossary entries together, and discuss what they have in common. Then guide students through the skill practice activities. For the strategy practice activity, pair students or complete it as a group.

DAY 2

Review the *Nonfiction Text Features* skill with students by showing the features you shared on Day 1. Point out the table of contents on page 78. Say: **This is an example of a nonfiction text feature called a *table of contents*. Raise a hand if you have seen a feature like this in a book before.** Read the instructions at the top of the page aloud. Then read the table of contents together. Remind students of the *Organization* strategy, which was taught during Week 3, and ask them to figure out how the table of contents is organized (sequentially; in page order; etc.). Before completing the skill practice activity, ask for volunteers to find this feature in several books you have on hand. Tell students that most books with separate sections or chapters will have a table of contents. Complete the skill practice activity together. For the strategy practice activity, pair students or complete it as a group.

DAY 3

Introduce the *Visual Information* skill to students. Explain that information can be given as words or as graphics, such as pictures, graphs, and maps, and that sometimes visual information is easier and quicker to understand than text. Then read the instructions at the top of the page aloud. Give students time to look at the ad. Then discuss what can be learned from the graphics alone. Ask for volunteers to read the words in the ad. Point out the words *Big Savings* in the burst, and ask students to explain the purpose of the burst (to get your attention). Direct students to complete the skill practice activity independently. Review the answers together. Then remind students of the *Determine Important Information* strategy and of the need to not be distracted by interesting information that may not be as important. Direct students to complete the strategy practice activity and to share their responses.

DAY 4

Review that *visual information* is the term for non-word features such as pictures, maps, and graphs. Ask students to name the type of visual shown on page 80 (circle chart; circle graph; pie chart). Tell them that the writer chose to use this form of organization and that the chart shows the daily activities of a girl named Maya. Give students time to study the chart. Then read the labels aloud together. If students have not had much experience interpreting circle/pie charts, you may wish to complete the skill practice activity together. For the strategy practice activity, pair students or complete it as a group.

DAY 5

Tell students they will practice both the *Nonfiction Text Features* and *Visual Information* skills. Remind students of the *Determine Important Information* strategy and tell them that when information is very important, it may be presented in several ways to make sure the reader understands it. Guide students to use both pictures and words to study the sign. Direct students to complete the activities, and review the answers together.

Daily Reading Comprehension • EMC 3452 • © Evan-Moor Corp.

READ THE GLOSSARY Think about where you might find a glossary.

Glossary

blood the red liquid that carries oxygen to different parts of the body

heart a muscle that pumps blood through the body

lungs the organs in the chest that are used for breathing

skeleton the bones that support the body

SKILL PRACTICE Read the question. Fill in the bubble next to the correct answer.

1. The words in the glossary would most likely be in a book about _____.

   Ⓐ what is inside Earth

   Ⓑ the human body

   Ⓒ pictures painted by artists

   Ⓓ planets around the sun

2. What does the glossary of a book tell the meaning of?

   Ⓐ important words

   Ⓑ pictures in the book

   Ⓒ the chapters of the book

   Ⓓ the names of the authors

3. The important words in the glossary _____.

   Ⓐ are in capital letters

   Ⓑ have pictures

   Ⓒ are in bold print

   Ⓓ are numbered

4. What helps you to find a word in a glossary?

   Ⓐ The words are numbered.

   Ⓑ The words are colored.

   Ⓒ The words are in big print.

   Ⓓ The words are in ABC order.

STRATEGY PRACTICE Tell a partner how a glossary could help you and when you might use it.

READ THE TABLE OF CONTENTS Think about where you would see information organized in this way.

Fruit Group 4

Vegetable Group 12

Grain Group 19

Meat Group 23

Milk Group 129

SKILL PRACTICE Read the question. Fill in the bubble next to the correct answer.

1. What title should be on the list above?
 Ⓐ Contents
 Ⓑ Glossary
 Ⓒ Chapter One
 Ⓓ About the Author

2. Each heading names one _____.
 Ⓐ page
 Ⓑ chapter
 Ⓒ picture
 Ⓓ meal

3. Which part begins on page 23?
 Ⓐ Milk Group
 Ⓑ Fruit Group
 Ⓒ Meat Group
 Ⓓ Grain Group

4. In which chapter would you find this sentence?
 Butter, yogurt, and cheese are in this food group.
 Ⓐ Milk Group
 Ⓑ Vegetable Group
 Ⓒ Fruit Group
 Ⓓ Grain Group

STRATEGY PRACTICE How does a table of contents help you find information? Tell a partner what you think.

Daily Reading Comprehension • EMC 3452 • © Evan-Moor Corp.

Name: _____

READ THE AD   Think about how the drawings help you understand the ad.

THIS WEEKEND ONLY!
Friday, Saturday, and Sunday
August 15–17

Big Savings!

Bert's School Supply • 3532 Pleasant Valley Drive

SKILL PRACTICE   Read the question. Fill in the bubble next to the correct answer.

1. What is for sale in the ad?

Ⓐ lunch foods

Ⓑ garden tools

Ⓒ party games

Ⓓ school things

2. Where is the sale happening?

Ⓐ August 14

Ⓑ for 3 days

Ⓒ at Bert's School Supply

Ⓓ in the newspaper

3. When is the sale happening?

Ⓐ 2 days only

Ⓑ 3 days only

Ⓒ on Saturday only

Ⓓ Monday through Friday

4. Where would you probably find the ad?

Ⓐ in the phone book

Ⓑ on TV

Ⓒ on a grocery store flyer

Ⓓ in a newspaper

STRATEGY PRACTICE   If you wanted to go to the sale, which two things would you have to know?

_____

_____

READ THE CHART Think about what the information in the circle chart shows.

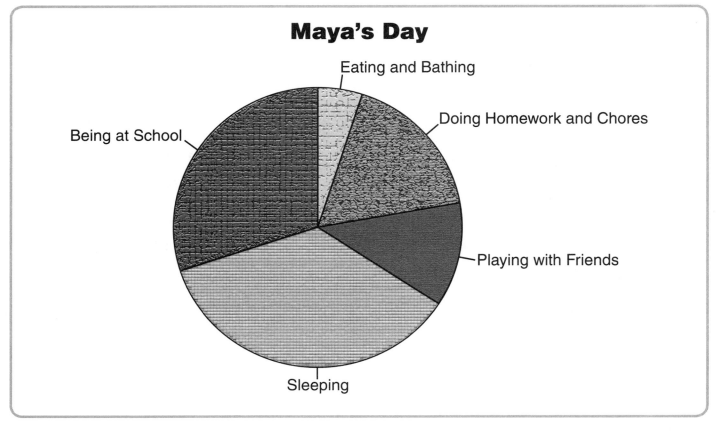

Maya's Day

- Eating and Bathing
- Doing Homework and Chores
- Being at School
- Playing with Friends
- Sleeping

SKILL PRACTICE Read the question. Fill in the bubble next to the correct answer.

1. What does the circle chart show?
   - Ⓐ who Maya's friends are
   - Ⓑ how Maya spends time
   - Ⓒ what Maya likes to read
   - Ⓓ where Maya's sisters go

2. Which activity takes the most time?
   - Ⓐ eating and bathing
   - Ⓑ playing with friends
   - Ⓒ being at school
   - Ⓓ sleeping

3. Which activity takes the least time?
   - Ⓐ doing homework and chores
   - Ⓑ playing with friends
   - Ⓒ eating and bathing
   - Ⓓ being at school

4. More than half of Maya's day is spent _____.
   - Ⓐ eating, bathing, and playing
   - Ⓑ doing homework and chores
   - Ⓒ being at school and sleeping
   - Ⓓ playing and doing homework and chores

STRATEGY PRACTICE Discuss with a partner why you think the writer used a circle chart to show the information instead of writing it in a paragraph.

READ THE SIGN Look carefully at the picture that goes with each group of words.

POOL RULES

 WATCH YOUR CHILDREN   NO FOOD OR DRINK

 DON'T SWIM ALONE   NO PETS IN POOL AREA

 NO DIVING   NO TOYS IN POOL

 NO RUNNING   HAVE FUN!

SKILL PRACTICE Read the question. Fill in the bubble next to the correct answer.

1. Which one tells what the sign is about?
   Ⓐ "Pool Rules"
   Ⓑ "Have Fun!"
   Ⓒ "Don't Swim Alone"
   Ⓓ "No Running"

2. What does this picture mean?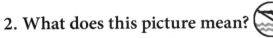
   Ⓐ "No Food or Drink"
   Ⓑ "No Running"
   Ⓒ "Don't Swim Alone"
   Ⓓ "No Diving"

3. Which picture means "No Pets in Pool Area"?
   Ⓐ
   Ⓑ
   Ⓒ
   Ⓓ

4. Which rule is least important for your safety?
   Ⓐ "No Pets in Pool Area"
   Ⓑ "Watch Your Children"
   Ⓒ "Have Fun!"
   Ⓓ "No Running"

STRATEGY PRACTICE What features helped you understand the important information?

_____

Main Idea and Details

Students look for the central idea or message of a passage or story. They also find details that best support the main idea.

Sequence

Students look for the order of events or steps in a process.

DAY 1

Review the *Main Idea and Details* skill with students. Say: **Remember that the *main idea* is what the passage is mostly about. Ideas that tell us more about the main idea are called *details*.** Read the instructions at the top of the page aloud. Say: **As good readers, we stop while reading and ask, *What is the most important idea of the part I just read?* When we do this, we are monitoring our comprehension** (taught during Week 6). **Good readers also know that the title can give a clue to the main idea.** Read the title together and speculate what "the tallest one" might be. Write students' responses on the board. Then have students read the passage. Ask them to evaluate their prereading speculations about the title. Then direct students to complete the skill practice activity, and review the answers together. After students complete the strategy practice activity, have volunteers share their responses.

DAY 2

Remind students of the *Main Idea and Details* skill. Read the instructions at the top of the page aloud. Have a student read the title aloud, and then ask the class what they are going to be reading about (bowling). Allow students to share what they know about bowling. List responses on the board. Remind students of the *Determine Important Information* strategy (taught during Week 4). Say: **It's important to notice which details tell the main things about bowling and which details are less important, even though they may be interesting.** Direct students to read the passage and to add any new information about bowling to the list on the board. Complete the skill practice activity and review the answers together. Then direct students to complete the strategy practice activity. Discuss students' responses, recognizing that there are more than two important sentences in the passage.

DAY 3

Ask students to recall the name of the skill good readers are using when they pay attention to the order in which events happen (the *Sequence* skill). Say: **We are going to read about how frogs start out as tiny creatures called *tadpoles* and grow into adult frogs. Remembering the sequence of how this happens will help you understand the information. Good readers stop while reading to monitor their comprehension. They ask themselves if they remember the sequence of events.** Direct students to read the passage and to complete the skill practice activity. Pair students to complete the strategy practice activity, reminding them to listen to make sure their partners tell the information in the correct sequence.

DAY 4

Write the words *First, Next, Then,* and *Last* on the board. Remind students of the *Sequence* skill. Say: **Writers often use certain words to help the reader understand the sequence in which things are happening. We call these words *signal words*. Let's read the signal words on the board together.** Then read the instructions at the top of the page and the title aloud. Tell students that passages that tell how to do something often use signal words so that the order of doing things is clear to the reader. Signal words help the reader to determine the important information in a passage. Direct students to read the passage and to notice signal words as they read. Then direct students to complete the activities. Review the answers together.

DAY 5

Tell students they will practice both the *Main Idea and Details* and *Sequence* skills as they read about something called the "water cycle." Remind students of the *Monitor Comprehension* strategy. Instruct them to stop reading after each paragraph to remind themselves of what they have read. Read the instructions at the top of the page aloud. After students have read the passage, ask them to relate what they read to the title ("In the water cycle, water goes around and around from one form to another."). Complete the activities and review the answers together.

Tell yourself what each paragraph is about.

The Tallest One

It was the summer of 2006. Two scientists were hiking in a California forest. The forest was filled with many tall redwood trees. The scientists were looking for the tallest ones. "Michael, get back here," one of them said. "Here is a really tall one." He was right! They named the tree Hyperion (hi-PAIR-ee-un).

To measure Hyperion, a man climbed all the way to the top. It took a long time. Hyperion's lowest branches are 200 feet above the ground. He used a bow and arrow to shoot ropes over those branches. Then he climbed up the trunk of the tree. He wore a helmet. He had a radio to talk to the people on the ground.

Up, up he climbed. The branches near the top were small. It was scary to go all the way up. But he did. When he got there, he dropped a tape measure down to the ground. Hyperion measured 379 feet tall. That's 70 feet taller than the Statue of Liberty! It is the tallest tree in the world.

SKILL PRACTICE   Read the question. Fill in the bubble next to the correct answer.

1. What is the passage mostly about?
   - Ⓐ measuring the tallest tree
   - Ⓑ using a rope to climb
   - Ⓒ hiking in the forest
   - Ⓓ shooting a bow and arrow

2. Why were the men in the forest?
   - Ⓐ to shoot a bow and arrow
   - Ⓑ to look for the tallest trees
   - Ⓒ to see how far they could hike
   - Ⓓ to see how high they could climb

3. What did the men use to learn the tree's size?
   - Ⓐ a bow and arrow
   - Ⓑ a radio
   - Ⓒ a statue
   - Ⓓ a tape measure

4. The climber used a radio to _____.
   - Ⓐ find his way out of the forest
   - Ⓑ listen to the news about trees
   - Ⓒ talk to the people on the ground
   - Ⓓ learn about the Statue of Liberty

STRATEGY PRACTICE   Write a question you had about the tallest tree that was answered in the passage.

_____

READ THE PASSAGE Notice which sentences tell details about bowling.

Let's Go Bowling!

It's a cold, rainy, winter day. You and your family are bored. You want to have some fun. You can't go outside. What <u>can</u> you do? Why not go bowling?

Drive to the bowling alley and park the car. Inside, put on bowling shoes. These shoes have special soles and are funny colors. Then choose a ball. Some balls are heavy. Others are light. The balls have three holes where you put your thumb and middle and ring fingers.

Next, find an empty lane. A lane looks like a long, wooden hallway. It has a ditch, called a gutter, along each side. At the far end are ten wooden pins. You must try to knock the pins down.

Pick up your ball and aim it at the pins. Roll the ball down the lane toward the pins. Hope it doesn't go in the gutter! Listen to the ball rumble as it rolls. *Crash!* It hits some of the pins. Down they fall. Hooray for you!

SKILL PRACTICE Read the question. Fill in the bubble next to the correct answer.

1. **What is the passage mostly about?**
   Ⓐ wooden pins
   Ⓑ an indoor sport
   Ⓒ a ball with three holes
   Ⓓ a family that is bored

2. **What do you try to do when you bowl?**
   Ⓐ slide as far as you can
   Ⓑ hit the pins with the ball
   Ⓒ stay out of the rain
   Ⓓ make noise with the ball

3. **Which one is an important idea in the passage?**
   Ⓐ Bowling balls make a lot of noise.
   Ⓑ There are gutters next to the lanes.
   Ⓒ People get bored when it rains.
   Ⓓ Bowling can be a fun thing to do.

4. **What does a lane look like?**
   Ⓐ a ditch
   Ⓑ a wooden pin
   Ⓒ a wooden hallway
   Ⓓ a small room

STRATEGY PRACTICE Underline two sentences in the passage that tell important details.

READ THE PASSAGE Notice the steps in how a tadpole grows into a frog.

Tadpole to Frog

The frog starts its life as a tadpole. Tadpoles look like tiny black or brown balls with tails. A new baby tadpole sticks itself to grass or weeds in the water.

One week later, the tadpole can swim. It zips back and forth with other tadpoles! It also grows some tiny teeth. All that swimming makes a tadpole hungry. It gobbles up a soft, green plant called algae (AL-gee).

When the tadpole is 6 to 9 weeks old, its body gets longer. It stops looking like a ball. It grows back legs first and then front legs. It starts to eat bugs.

As the tadpole grows, its tail gets shorter. Its face gets longer like a frog's. Soon the tiny tadpole has become a fat, little frog! By the time it is 16 weeks old, it can jump onto land.

SKILL PRACTICE Read the question. Fill in the bubble next to the correct answer.

1. What does a tadpole look like first?
   - Ⓐ a tiny brown or black ball
   - Ⓑ a tiny black bug
   - Ⓒ a piece of grass
   - Ⓓ a little frog

2. When does a tadpole begin to eat algae?
   - Ⓐ after it goes on land
   - Ⓑ after it grows legs
   - Ⓒ after its tail gets shorter
   - Ⓓ after it grows tiny teeth

3. What happens before a tadpole eats bugs?
   - Ⓐ It grows legs.
   - Ⓑ It becomes a frog.
   - Ⓒ It jumps onto land.
   - Ⓓ Its tail gets shorter.

4. What does the passage tell about last?
   - Ⓐ eating soft, green plants
   - Ⓑ growing back and front legs
   - Ⓒ jumping onto land
   - Ⓓ swimming with other tadpoles

STRATEGY PRACTICE Tell a partner what happens as a tadpole becomes a frog.

READ THE PASSAGE Look for signal words that tell you the order of events.

How to Wash a Car

Washing a car is fun on a hot summer day. First, you must close the car windows. You don't want to get the seats wet! Next, make sure that the hose is long enough. It has to reach the car. Then, turn on the hose and get ready to spray. Spray water on the windows. Spray water on the doors. Spray water on the bumpers and wheels.

Next, use a big, soapy sponge to rub the car all over. Rub, rub, rub! Rub the doors. Rub the windows. Rub the front and back.

Then, it's time to rinse. It takes some time to get all the soap off. Use the hose to wash off all the soap. Start at the roof and go down. Soapy water will run down the windows. It will run down onto the ground.

Last, get an old towel. Wipe the car to get it dry. Stand back and see yourself in the shiny paint. Wow! Good job!

SKILL PRACTICE Read the question. Fill in the bubble next to the correct answer.

1. **Which of these steps happens first?**
   - Ⓐ Get the car wet.
   - Ⓑ Turn on the hose.
   - Ⓒ Get the car soapy.
   - Ⓓ Close the windows.

2. **Right after you rub the car with soap, you _____.**
   - Ⓐ dry it with a towel
   - Ⓑ rinse it with water from a hose
   - Ⓒ close all the windows
   - Ⓓ look at yourself in the shiny paint

3. **When are the windows washed?**
   - Ⓐ after the car is shiny
   - Ⓑ before the car is soapy
   - Ⓒ before the car is sprayed
   - Ⓓ when the car is washed

4. **Which of these is used last?**
   - Ⓐ soap
   - Ⓑ water
   - Ⓒ a towel
   - Ⓓ a sponge

STRATEGY PRACTICE Underline the signal words in the first paragraph that tell the steps for washing a car.

READ THE PASSAGE   Remember the main ideas and the order in which they happen.

Around and Around

When it rains, water falls from clouds to the ground. How does the water get into the sky? It is something called the water cycle.

There is always water in the air, but you can't always see it. It's called water vapor. The sun heats up water in rivers, lakes, and oceans. The water turns into water vapor. It goes into the air.

High in the sky, it is cold. When water vapor gets cold, it becomes water again. You can see this happen when you have a cold drink on a warm day. Water is on the outside of the glass. Did the glass leak? No, water vapor in the air turned to water when it touched the cold glass.

Millions of water drops come together in the sky. They make clouds. Pretty soon there is more water than the clouds can hold. Then the water falls to Earth.

Rain falls back into the oceans, lakes, and rivers. The sun turns it into water vapor. The water cycle starts all over again.

SKILL PRACTICE   Read the question. Fill in the bubble next to the correct answer.

1. **What is the passage mostly about?**

   Ⓐ oceans, lakes, and rivers

   Ⓑ how clouds are made

   Ⓒ how water keeps going in a cycle

   Ⓓ how the sun makes water vapor

2. **What happens when clouds cannot hold any more water?**

   Ⓐ The sun dries them.

   Ⓑ Water falls to Earth.

   Ⓒ Water vapor goes into the air.

   Ⓓ Water drops come together.

3. **What happens just before clouds are formed?**

   Ⓐ The sun shines on the ocean.

   Ⓑ Water vapor rises into the air.

   Ⓒ Water falls back to Earth.

   Ⓓ Water drops start to come together.

4. **What do you think a "cycle" is?**

   Ⓐ something that keeps going around

   Ⓑ something that has water in it

   Ⓒ something that never happens

   Ⓓ something that is always new

STRATEGY PRACTICE   In your own words, tell a partner how water from the air falls to Earth.

Cause and Effect
Students practice the skill by looking for what happens (the effect) and why it happens (the cause).

Fact and Opinion
Students determine whether parts of the passage can be proved (facts) or represent what someone thinks or feels (opinions).

DAY 1

Review the *Cause and Effect* skill with students. Walk to the light switch and ask them what will happen if you flip the switch (lights will turn off). Say: **Flipping the switch is the cause. The lights turning off is the effect.** Tell students they will read about a class that decided to share with others. Read the instructions at the top of the page aloud. Remind students of the *Visualization* strategy, which was taught during Week 2. Tell students that making a mental image of what happens is a good way to picture the causes and effects in a passage. Then have students read the passage. When students have finished, direct them to complete the skill and strategy practice activities. Review the answers together.

DAY 2

Remind students of the *Cause and Effect* skill. Tell students they will read about a boy whose actions cause something unpleasant to happen to him. Remind students of the *Organization* strategy, which was taught during Week 3. Tell students that writers may organize their stories to have several causes and several effects, and that good readers pay attention to what happens and the reason it happens. Read the instructions at the top of the page aloud. Then have students read the passage. When students have finished, direct them to complete the skill and strategy practice activities. Review the answers together.

DAY 3

Review the *Fact and Opinion* skill with students. Say: **A fact can be proved. An opinion is what someone thinks or believes. If I tell you that some playgrounds have slides, is that a fact or an opinion?** (fact) **If I tell you that slides are the most fun piece of equipment on a playground, is that a fact or an opinion?** (opinion) **It's an opinion because it is only what I think. You may think something different.** Read the instructions at the top of the page aloud. Then remind students of the *Visualization* strategy. Direct students to read the passage and to complete the skill and strategy practice activities. Review the answers together, allowing students to share their answers to the strategy practice activity.

DAY 4

Remind students of the *Fact and Opinion* skill and the *Organization* strategy. Say: **One way writers make a passage interesting is to mix facts and opinions together. Just because you read a sentence that is a fact, you shouldn't think that the next sentence will also be a fact. Writers may also give facts and opinions about one thing first and then give facts and opinions about another thing. Good readers ask,** *Is this a fact or an opinion? What is the fact or opinion about?* Then read the instructions at the top of the page aloud. Remind students of the *Visualization* strategy as a way to help them determine what can be proved and what someone thinks. Direct students to read the passage and to complete the skill and strategy practice activities. Review the answers together.

DAY 5

Tell students they will practice the *Cause and Effect* and *Fact and Opinion* skills. Tell them they are going to read about some things that happen in a classroom on a particular day. Say: **You will need to read carefully to find different cause-and-effect relationships, as well as examples of facts and opinions.** Remind students that using the *Visualization* strategy can help them to see the causes, effects, facts, and opinions in a passage. Then have students read the passage. When students have finished, direct them to complete the skill and strategy practice activities. Review the answers together.

READ THE PASSAGE Pay attention to the reasons people do things.

Sharing Music

The students in Mr. Caro's classroom were excited. They were getting ready for the winter holidays. They made lacy paper snowflakes to hang in the windows. They planned their holiday party. They learned cheerful holiday songs and sang them together each day.

"You sound very good!" said Mr. Caro. "I have an idea. The holidays are a good time for giving. Would you like to share your music?"

"Yes!" said the children. And so they did. They went to a hospital near their school. They sang for the people there. The doctors and nurses smiled. The sick people smiled, too. They all clapped their hands and thanked the children.

The class walked from the hospital to a home where older people go to live. They sang joyfully as they walked through the halls. The men and women who lived there smiled and waved from their rooms. The music had made their day special.

SKILL PRACTICE Read the question. Fill in the bubble next to the correct answer.

1. **Why is the class excited?**

   Ⓐ The holidays are coming up.

   Ⓑ The first snow has fallen.

   Ⓒ A music show is in town.

   Ⓓ Mr. Caro is having a birthday party.

2. **Mr. Caro asks the students to share their music because he _____.**

   Ⓐ wants the class to leave school

   Ⓑ wants to walk to the hospital

   Ⓒ has a friend who is sick

   Ⓓ thinks they sound good

3. **Why do the doctors thank the class?**

   Ⓐ The class makes the sick people well.

   Ⓑ The class teaches music to others.

   Ⓒ The class sings songs at the hospital.

   Ⓓ The class put snowflakes in the windows.

4. **Why are people smiling and waving?**

   Ⓐ The doctors tell the people to wave.

   Ⓑ The people like the children's singing.

   Ⓒ The people want to share.

   Ⓓ The people live near the hospital.

STRATEGY PRACTICE Underline the sentences that helped you see the people who listened to the children singing.

Look for reasons why Kobe has an accident.

Kobe Learns a Lesson

Kobe rolled into the driveway on his skateboard. Dad was just getting home from work. He stepped out of the car. "Hi, Dad!" said Kobe.

"Hey, son. I see that your skateboard is wobbling. Let's take a look at the wheels."

"Not now, Dad," Kobe said. "I want to call Bill. He has a new video game."

On Saturday morning, Kobe's brother was wearing a soccer shirt. "Dad says your skateboard needs some work," he said to Kobe. "I can help you fix it. I can help you before my game."

"That's OK," said Kobe. "I can fix it later." He was watching a TV show. When the show ended, Kobe went outside. He hopped onto his skateboard. Then he took off toward Bill's house. *Wobble, wobble, bump!* Kobe fell to the ground. Ouch! He had hurt his knee. Kobe limped home with his broken skateboard. He had learned a lesson.

SKILL PRACTICE Read the question. Fill in the bubble next to the correct answer.

1. Why does Kobe's father want to look at the wheels?

   Ⓐ His father came home from work.
   Ⓑ Kobe said the wheels do not work.
   Ⓒ Kobe fell off his skateboard.
   Ⓓ His father sees the wheels wobble.

2. Why does Kobe want to call Bill?

   Ⓐ Bill has a new video game.
   Ⓑ Bill is playing soccer.
   Ⓒ Bill has a new skateboard.
   Ⓓ Bill is watching a TV show.

3. How does Kobe's brother know the board needs work?

   Ⓐ He saw the board.
   Ⓑ Their dad told him.
   Ⓒ He rode the board.
   Ⓓ Their friend told him.

4. Kobe gets hurt because _____.

   Ⓐ he did not fix his board
   Ⓑ he hops off his board
   Ⓒ his board hits a soccer ball
   Ⓓ he rolls his board into a parked car

STRATEGY PRACTICE Underline the chances Kobe had to fix his skateboard.

READ THE PASSAGE Look for facts and opinions about the playground.

A Super Playground

Last summer I visited my aunt and uncle. They are really cool! They had something exciting planned for each day. But the day we went to Dennis the Menace Playground was the very best.

There is so much neat stuff at this playground! When you go in the gate, you see a real steam engine. You can climb up the ladder and go inside the cab. I pretended that I was running the train.

Aunt Peg said I was brave to go on the climbing wall. It's nine feet high. We all went down the giant, curvy green slide. But Uncle Ed wouldn't run across the swinging bridge. He said it was too scary. I felt like I was a jungle explorer.

You won't believe how you get a drink of water on the playground. You put your head in a lion's mouth! But don't worry. The lion is fake.

There are a lot of other really fun things at Dennis the Menace Playground. You should go see for yourself!

SKILL PRACTICE Read the question. Fill in the bubble next to the correct answer.

1. Which one is a fact?
   Ⓐ The swinging bridge is scary.
   Ⓑ The climbing wall is nine feet high.
   Ⓒ Aunt Peg and Uncle Ed are cool.
   Ⓓ This playground is super fun.

2. Which one is an opinion?
   Ⓐ The person telling the story is brave.
   Ⓑ The giant slide is green.
   Ⓒ The lion is not real.
   Ⓓ You can climb into a steam engine.

3. Which one is an opinion?
   Ⓐ Peg and Ed planned things to do.
   Ⓑ You can get a drink of water.
   Ⓒ This playground is really fun.
   Ⓓ There is a swinging bridge.

4. The person telling the story _____.
   Ⓐ is ready to go home
   Ⓑ is afraid of lions
   Ⓒ thinks you should go to this place
   Ⓓ is a jungle explorer

STRATEGY PRACTICE Underline the part of the passage that made the most interesting picture in your mind.

Look for two different opinions about sports.

Which Sport Is for You?

My big sister Marta loves team sports! She plays on a soccer team in the summer. In the winter, she plays volleyball and basketball. Marta says team sports help her stay healthy. Running, jumping, and throwing balls is good exercise. She says that sports are good for the mind, too. Players must make choices. They have to think fast.

Marta thinks team sports are the best. Team sports teach you how to play with others. Team sports also teach people how to be fair. They learn good ways to act when they lose, too.

I like swimming and bike riding. You can do them by yourself or with a friend. You don't have to wait for a team to get together.

What do you think? Which sport is for you?

SKILL PRACTICE   Read the question. Fill in the bubble next to the correct answer.

1. **Which one is an opinion about playing basketball?**
   Ⓐ It is exercise.
   Ⓑ It is better than swimming.
   Ⓒ You play with others.
   Ⓓ You play with a ball.

2. **Which one is a fact?**
   Ⓐ Soccer is a fun sport.
   Ⓑ Swimming is better than soccer.
   Ⓒ You can ride a bike by yourself.
   Ⓓ Team sports are the best.

3. **Which one is an opinion?**
   Ⓐ Soccer is a team sport.
   Ⓑ Team sports are good for you.
   Ⓒ You play some sports outside.
   Ⓓ Sometimes teams lose.

4. **Which one is <u>not</u> a fact about bike riding?**
   Ⓐ It is better than volleyball.
   Ⓑ You can do it by yourself.
   Ⓒ You do not need a team to do it.
   Ⓓ It is exercise.

STRATEGY PRACTICE   Circle the part that tells about team sports. Draw a box around the part that tells about individual sports.

READ THE PASSAGE Look for reasons things happen. Notice facts and opinions.

Class Helpers

Mrs. Lopez looks around her class and smiles. She is the teacher, but today she isn't teaching. Today her students are helping each other learn.

Sal and Hannah are sitting across from each other. They are helping each other learn math. Sal holds up a flashcard. It is made of thick white paper. Sal sees the number 8 on his side of the card. Hannah reads "17 minus 9" on her side. "Eight," says Hannah.

"Right!" says Sal. Then he holds up another flashcard.

Toby and Juan sit on pillows in the book nook. They are practicing their readers' theater parts. "I like the way you read that part," said Toby. "You made it funny."

The students in Mrs. Lopez's class know something important. Learning is easier and more fun when you do it together.

SKILL PRACTICE Read the question. Fill in the bubble next to the correct answer.

1. Mrs. Lopez smiles because _____.

   Ⓐ the class is very quiet

   Ⓑ she made the flashcards

   Ⓒ she knows all number facts

   Ⓓ her students are working together

2. Toby thinks Juan's part is interesting because _____.

   Ⓐ it is a good story

   Ⓑ he likes Juan

   Ⓒ Juan reads it well

   Ⓓ he and Juan sit together

3. Which one is a fact?

   Ⓐ Sitting on pillows is better than sitting on chairs.

   Ⓑ Math is more fun than reading.

   Ⓒ Mrs. Lopez is the best teacher.

   Ⓓ Sal's flashcard is made of thick paper.

4. Which one is an opinion?

   Ⓐ Toby likes the way Juan reads.

   Ⓑ Flashcards are made of paper.

   Ⓒ Mrs. Lopez is a teacher.

   Ⓓ Hannah gets the right answer.

STRATEGY PRACTICE Underline a part in the passage you saw clearly in your mind.

Compare and Contrast

Students look for similarities and differences between two or more people or things.

Make Inferences

Students look for clues in the passage and draw upon their own experience to understand information that is not directly stated.

DAY 1

Review the *Compare and Contrast* skill with students. Say: **When we compare and contrast two or more things, we look for how they are alike and different.** Pick two objects in the classroom—a globe and a playground ball, for example—and have students compare and contrast them. Read the instructions at the top of the page aloud. Remind students of the *Ask Questions* strategy, which was taught during Week 5. Say: **As good readers, we ask questions that we want to find the answers to before we begin reading.** Brainstorm and list questions that students have about the passage. Then direct students to read the passage and to complete the skill practice activity. Review the answers together, having students locate the parts of the passage that confirm their answers. For the strategy practice activity, review the list of questions generated before reading. Mark questions that were answered by the passage. Direct students to choose one of those questions and copy it on the line in the strategy practice section.

DAY 2

Remind students of the *Compare and Contrast* skill. Tell them they will read about two pet cats. Then read the instructions at the top of the page aloud. Remind students of the *Monitor Comprehension* strategy, which was taught during Week 6. Draw a Venn diagram on the board, and tell students that using a diagram is a good way to record how two things are the same or different. Read the passage aloud together. Stop after each paragraph to record the cats' similarities and differences on the diagram. After reading the passage and completing the diagram, direct students to complete the skill practice activity independently, using the diagram to confirm their answer choices. Review the answers together. For the strategy practice activity, pair students or complete it as a group.

DAY 3

Review the *Make Inferences* skill with students. Say: **When we make an inference, we use clues from the passage and our own experience to figure out information that we haven't been told.** Then say: **Imagine you see your friend's bike lying on the ground. Your friend is sitting on the ground nearby, holding his knee. What do you suppose happened?** (friend fell off bike) **How do you know?** (bike and friend on ground; friend's knee hurt) Read the instructions at the top of the page aloud. Then remind students of the *Ask Questions* strategy. Tell them that asking questions about what they have just read will help them remember and understand the passage. Then direct students to read the passage and to complete the skill and strategy practice activities. Review the answers together.

DAY 4

Remind students of the *Make Inferences* skill. Ask students what they know about the White House. List students' ideas on the board. Tell them they are going to read about how some students like themselves helped to plant a garden at the White House. Read the instructions at the top of the page aloud. Remind students of the *Monitor Comprehension* strategy. Tell them as they read, they should pause to make sure they can tell what they read. If they find that their minds have wandered, they should reread. Direct students to read the passage and to complete the skill practice activity. Review the answers together. For the strategy practice activity, pair students or complete it as a group.

DAY 5

Tell students they will practice both the *Compare and Contrast* and *Make Inferences* skills. Read the instructions at the top of the page aloud. Remind students of the *Ask Questions* strategy. On the line provided for the strategy practice section, have students write a question they would like to ask about animals' eyes. Direct students to read the passage and to complete the skill practice activity. For the strategy practice activity, allow students to share their question with a partner and discuss whether or not they found the answer in the passage.

Daily Reading Comprehension • EMC 3452 • © Evan-Moor Corp.

READ THE PASSAGE Find out how the two kinds of ducks are alike and different.

Dippers and Divers

Most ducks are either dippers or divers. Dippers float in shallow water. Many live near ponds. Some people call them "puddle ducks." Dippers stick their heads underwater. Their tails point high in the air. They are looking for food. Dippers eat a lot of plants. They find them on the bottom of the pond. They eat bugs and small fish, too. Dippers can walk and run well on land.

You'll see divers on deep lakes and rivers or on the sea. They can dive deep for their food. They come back up with clams, crabs, and fish. Divers have shorter legs and bigger feet than dippers. They can swim very fast, but they cannot walk very well.

A dipper can leap up out of the water to begin flying. Divers cannot leap. They are too heavy. They flap their wings and run along on the water. Then they take off like a plane.

SKILL PRACTICE Read the question. Fill in the bubble next to the correct answer.

1. Dippers and divers are both _____.

   Ⓐ ducks

   Ⓑ ponds

   Ⓒ planes

   Ⓓ bugs

2. One way dippers and divers are different is that dippers _____.

   Ⓐ have bigger feet

   Ⓑ have shorter legs

   Ⓒ stay in shallow water

   Ⓓ eat clams from the sea

3. Dippers and divers both _____.

   Ⓐ walk well on land

   Ⓑ find food in water

   Ⓒ take off like planes

   Ⓓ live in shallow ponds

4. What can a dipper do that a diver <u>cannot</u>?

   Ⓐ swim very fast

   Ⓑ eat a crab

   Ⓒ dive deep for food

   Ⓓ walk well on land

STRATEGY PRACTICE What is a question you had that was answered by the passage?

_____

_____

READ THE PASSAGE Find out how the two cats are alike and different.

Salt and Pepper

My cats are funny. They rest in the sun all day. When we get home, they run to greet us just like a pair of dogs. Salt is yellow and white. His fur is shiny. His eyes are golden. Pepper is gray and fluffy. His eyes are green like fresh grass.

Salt is smart, but Pepper is not. Salt takes care of Pepper. He keeps him from bothering the skunk that lives in the woods nearby. He keeps him from sleeping in the middle of the road where he could get hit by a car.

Salt curls up in a ball when he sleeps. He puts one paw over his face. Pepper stretches out on his back. He puts his arms over his head.

Both cats like to be petted on their heads. Both purr when we feed them. They run to the kitchen when we call. Then they put their heads down side by side to enjoy their dinners.

SKILL PRACTICE Read the question. Fill in the bubble next to the correct answer.

1. Salt and Pepper are both _____.
   - Ⓐ cars
   - Ⓑ cats
   - Ⓒ dogs
   - Ⓓ skunks

2. Salt and Pepper both _____.
   - Ⓐ have gray fur
   - Ⓑ have gold eyes
   - Ⓒ purr when they eat
   - Ⓓ sleep on their backs

3. What does Salt do that Pepper does <u>not</u>?
   - Ⓐ rests all day in the sun
   - Ⓑ bothers a nearby skunk
   - Ⓒ runs to greet people
   - Ⓓ curls up in a ball to sleep

4. What is one way the cats are different?
   - Ⓐ Salt is smarter.
   - Ⓑ Pepper is shinier.
   - Ⓒ Pepper eats dinner alone.
   - Ⓓ Pepper takes care of the skunk.

STRATEGY PRACTICE Tell a partner about the two cats in the passage.

READ THE PASSAGE   Look for details in the passage that tell you autumn is coming.

It's Autumn

Summer is over. In some places, the days grow cool. We put away our swimsuits. We take out sweaters for chilly mornings. The air feels crisp and fresh. The pumpkins in the field are big, round, and orange like the sun. The apples are ready to eat.

The leaves on some of the trees change color. Some turn red. Others turn yellow or orange. They are bright and amazing to see! Where did the colors come from? They were there all along. When the days get colder, the green color on the leaves goes away. We see bright new colors.

The leaves dry out and fall from the trees. They crunch under our feet as we walk. We rake them into great big piles. We jump into the piles with our friends!

SKILL PRACTICE   Read the question. Fill in the bubble next to the correct answer.

1. **What probably happens to apples and pumpkins in autumn?**

   Ⓐ They fall from the trees.

   Ⓑ They dry out.

   Ⓒ They become ripe.

   Ⓓ They are raked into big piles.

2. **Which of these would most likely describe autumn leaves?**

   Ⓐ pretty

   Ⓑ dry

   Ⓒ round

   Ⓓ chilly

3. **Why do you think leaves are not bright colors in summer?**

   Ⓐ because they are not ripe yet

   Ⓑ because green hides the other colors

   Ⓒ because green is better for summer

   Ⓓ because they have not been raked into piles

4. **Why do you think the children jump into leaves?**

   Ⓐ to hide

   Ⓑ to dry them

   Ⓒ to get warm

   Ⓓ to have fun

STRATEGY PRACTICE   Write a question you have about the passage. Have a partner answer it.

READ THE PASSAGE   Find out why a garden was planted at the White House.

White House Garden

How would you like to visit the White House? The president's family lives there. A group of students were lucky. They went to the White House one spring. They helped the First Lady plant her garden. They planted seeds for lettuce and peas. They planted beans and broccoli, too. While they worked, the First Lady told them about healthful food. She said that eating well is one way they can take good care of their bodies.

The seeds that the children planted grew into plants. The plants grew and grew all summer long. In the fall, the children went back to the garden. It was time to pick the vegetables. The children picked a lot of lettuce. They picked other vegetables, too. Then they helped cook a meal in the White House kitchen. When it was ready, they all ate at a long table on the grass. They had helped grow and cook a wonderful feast!

SKILL PRACTICE   Read the question. Fill in the bubble next to the correct answer.

1. You could tell that the First Lady probably _____.

   Ⓐ cooks a lot

   Ⓑ eats only peas

   Ⓒ lives in her garden

   Ⓓ cares about children

2. The students who went to the White House most likely _____.

   Ⓐ were hungry

   Ⓑ worked very hard

   Ⓒ wanted to go home

   Ⓓ ate only lettuce

3. The First Lady probably planted a garden because she _____.

   Ⓐ likes broccoli best

   Ⓑ wants kids to cook

   Ⓒ wants children to eat healthful food

   Ⓓ does not like food from a store

4. The children who helped in the garden probably _____.

   Ⓐ felt proud

   Ⓑ like vegetables

   Ⓒ taught others to cook

   Ⓓ live at the White House

STRATEGY PRACTICE   Tell a partner what the children did in the White House garden in the spring.

Daily Reading Comprehension • EMC 3452 • © Evan-Moor Corp.

READ THE PASSAGE   Find out how animals' eyes are alike and different.

Animals' Eyes

Different animals' eyes work in different ways. Their eyes help them find food. Their eyes also help keep them safe by seeing danger.

Horses, sheep, and giraffes have eyes on the sides of their heads. They can see wide spaces while they eat. They can watch for signs of danger. A giraffe can see a lion several miles away!

Hunting birds such as eagles and hawks can see things far away. They can see their food from high in a tree or when they are flying. An eagle can spot a rabbit from a mile away. It can see the smallest move the rabbit makes.

Some animals sleep all day. They are awake at night. They must be able to see in the dark. Owls and tigers are two animals that see well in the dark.

The eyes each animal has are best for that animal. An animal's eyes help it live.

SKILL PRACTICE   Read the question. Fill in the bubble next to the correct answer.

1. Horses and sheep both have eyes _____.
   Ⓐ on the sides of their heads
   Ⓑ that do not see well
   Ⓒ that can see in the dark
   Ⓓ in the front of their heads

2. Eyes help some animals _____.
   Ⓐ run fast
   Ⓑ hunt
   Ⓒ sleep
   Ⓓ stay awake

3. One way tigers are different from us is that they can _____.
   Ⓐ eat when it is dark
   Ⓑ see all the way around themselves
   Ⓒ see well in darkness
   Ⓓ see things far away

4. Owls and tigers both _____.
   Ⓐ need sunlight to see
   Ⓑ hunt at night
   Ⓒ sleep all night
   Ⓓ eat in the daytime

STRATEGY PRACTICE   What question about animals' eyes would you like to ask?

_____

Character and Setting

Students study a passage to better understand who or what is at the center of the action and when and where the action takes place.

Fantasy and Reality

Students identify which things in the passage could or could not happen in real life.

DAY 1

Review the *Character and Setting* skill with students. Say: **The character is who a story or passage is mostly about. The setting is where and when a passage or story takes place.** Select a story students are familiar with and ask them to identify the character and setting (e.g., The characters in "The Three Billy Goats Gruff" are the three goats and the troll; the setting is a bridge over a stream.). Read the instructions at the top of the page aloud. Then remind students of the *Make Connections* strategy, which was taught during Week 1. Say: **It is easier to understand what the characters do and how they feel when you recall similar things that you may have done or seen.** Direct students to read the passage and to complete the skill practice activity. Review the answers together. For the strategy practice activity, pair students or complete it as a group.

DAY 2

Remind students of the *Character and Setting* skill. Tell students they are going to read about an adventure a boy has with his dad. Read the instructions at the top of the page aloud. Then remind students of the *Visualization* strategy, which was taught during Week 2. Say: **Making a mental picture of the characters and setting will help you understand and remember what you read.** Direct students to read the passage and to complete the skill practice activity. Review the answers together. For the strategy practice activity, pair students or complete it as a group.

DAY 3

Review the *Fantasy and Reality* skill with students. Say: **When something happens in a story that could happen or exist in real life, it is reality. Things that could not happen or exist in real life are fantasy. We are going to read a story about a family that is camping in their backyard. Does that sound like something that could happen?** (yes) Remind students of the *Make Connections* strategy, and tell them to notice things in the story that are similar to things they have done. Read the instructions at the top of the page aloud, and point out that there must be something in the story that is fantasy. Direct students to read the passage and to complete the skill and strategy practice activities. Review the answers together, allowing students to read aloud the sentence they underlined in the passage.

DAY 4

Remind students of the *Fantasy and Reality* skill. Read the instructions at the top of the page aloud, and point out that there must be something in the passage that is fantasy. Then read the title of the passage aloud. Ask students to speculate on what they will read about and what might be fantasy. Remind students to use the *Visualization* strategy to help them form mental pictures about what is happening. Direct students to read the passage and to complete the skill practice activity. Review the answers together. For the strategy practice activity, pair students or complete it as a group.

DAY 5

Tell students they will practice both the *Character and Setting* and *Fantasy and Reality* skills. Review the skills if necessary, and then read the instructions at the top of the page aloud. Remind students to make connections between themselves and the characters and events in order to better understand the story. Then have students read the passage. When students have finished, direct them to complete the skill and strategy practice activities. Review the answers together.

READ THE PASSAGE Look for words that tell how the characters feel.

River Rafting

Aya and her family drove to the river. A guide was waiting for them there. "Hi, I'm Matt," he said. "Here are your wet suits. The water is very cold!" Aya and her brother, Taro, pulled on their wet suits and life vests. They could hardly wait to begin. The children's father was eager, too. Their mother was not so sure.

"Why am I doing this?" she asked. She was very nervous.

"For fun!" said the children. "Don't worry, Mom. It will be great." They climbed into the raft and sat up on its sides. The guide gave everyone a paddle. He held an extra long paddle and sat in the back of the raft.

"Here we go!" said Matt, as they pushed off from the shore. The water sparkled in the warm sunshine, and the pine trees along the shore smelled fresh. Matt guided the raft through places where the water was bumpy. The children laughed and screamed as the raft went over the bumps.

"Woohoo!" shouted their mother. "This is fun!"

SKILL PRACTICE Read the question. Fill in the bubble next to the correct answer.

1. Matt seems very _____.
   Ⓐ shy
   Ⓑ angry
   Ⓒ funny
   Ⓓ friendly

2. Aya and Taro are ready to _____.
   Ⓐ have fun
   Ⓑ go home
   Ⓒ save their mother
   Ⓓ laugh at their father

3. Which word describes the activity the family did?
   Ⓐ dirty
   Ⓑ dark
   Ⓒ pretty
   Ⓓ exciting

4. Which one describes how Mom's feelings changed?
   Ⓐ from bored to interested
   Ⓑ from scared to happy
   Ⓒ from brave to frightened
   Ⓓ from eager to worried

STRATEGY PRACTICE Tell a partner about a time you were afraid at first but then had fun.

READ THE PASSAGE Picture in your mind the place where the characters are.

Across the Bridge

My name is Niel. I live in San Francisco. It is a hilly city. Up and down the car goes as we drive to the bay. Dad parks, and we get out. We are going to walk across the bridge!

The Golden Gate Bridge is beautiful. It is made of metal and is painted orange. It is almost two miles long. There are lanes for cars driving in and out of the city. There are sidewalks for walkers and bike riders.

It sure is windy up here! I'm glad we brought our jackets. Look! We're as high as the sea gulls. The water in the bay far below is deep blue. It is dotted with white sailboats. I can see the city buildings on the shore. I can see a big island and a small island.

It takes almost an hour for Dad and me to walk across the bridge. My uncle is waiting for us there. He has brought a picnic lunch. What a perfect day!

SKILL PRACTICE Read the question. Fill in the bubble next to the correct answer.

1. **Which set of words describe the bridge?**
   Ⓐ short, wooden, orange
   Ⓑ short, wooden, red
   Ⓒ long, metal, orange
   Ⓓ long, metal, red

2. **From the bridge, Niel sees _____.**
   Ⓐ the car
   Ⓑ a picnic
   Ⓒ his uncle
   Ⓓ two islands

3. **How does Niel feel about the walk?**
   Ⓐ He is too tired to have fun.
   Ⓑ He enjoys it.
   Ⓒ He is angry.
   Ⓓ He is a little bit scared.

4. **When Niel says, "What a perfect day!" it shows that he _____.**
   Ⓐ had plenty of lunch
   Ⓑ had a great time
   Ⓒ is ready to go home
   Ⓓ is tired from walking

STRATEGY PRACTICE Describe the Golden Gate Bridge to a partner.

READ THE PASSAGE   Notice where the passage becomes fantasy.

Backyard Camp-out

Ross and Dano pitched their tent. They were having a backyard camp-out. Dad cooked hot dogs on the grill. Mom made a fruit salad. They ate at the picnic table.

The sky grew dark, but the moon was full. It glowed with a silvery light. The boys crawled into their sleeping bags. Ross told stories about magic until they fell asleep. That night, both boys dreamed they were flying.

When the boys woke up, the sun was high in the sky. They unzipped the tent flap and stepped out. "Where are we?" asked Dano. He couldn't believe what he saw. Their tent was next to a lake. Their parents were sitting in chairs beside it.

"Good morning!" said Mom. "Your pancakes are ready."

"Hurry up and eat," said Dad. "Let's take the boat out and see if the fish are biting today." Ross and Dano stared at each other.

"I hope those pancakes are real," said Dano. "I'm hungry!"

SKILL PRACTICE   Read the question. Fill in the bubble next to the correct answer.

1. **Which one is make-believe?**
   Ⓐ sleeping bags
   Ⓑ moving by magic
   Ⓒ a full moon
   Ⓓ pancakes for breakfast

2. **How do the parents act?**
   Ⓐ afraid of the lake
   Ⓑ angry with the boys
   Ⓒ like nothing is strange
   Ⓓ surprised by the change

3. **Which one is not real?**
   Ⓐ a picnic table
   Ⓑ a family dinner
   Ⓒ a dad who cooks hot dogs
   Ⓓ a tent that moves while you sleep

4. **The boys stare at each other because _____.**
   Ⓐ they are not in the backyard now
   Ⓑ they do not like pancakes
   Ⓒ their parents are there
   Ⓓ they do not own a boat

STRATEGY PRACTICE   Underline a sentence in the passage that reminds you of something you have done or a way you have felt.

READ THE PASSAGE Ask yourself what could and could <u>not</u> happen.

Like a Fish

The summer days were long and hot. Sarah went to the pool at the park nearly every day. The clear blue water felt nice and cool. Sarah swam and swam. Sometimes she stayed until the pool closed for the day.

She had been in the water so much lately that Sarah felt like a fish. Back and forth in the lane she swam. She pretended that she was a mermaid. She thought about ships and sunken treasure. She thought about whales and dolphins. Back and forth she swam.

Suddenly, Sarah realized that she was breathing underwater! "Am I dreaming?" she asked herself. "Can this be real?" It was! She could breathe like a fish!

Splash! The lifeguard jumped into the pool and pulled Sarah over to the edge. "Are you OK?" he asked. "You held your breath underwater for so long that I started to worry."

"I can breathe underwater!" Sarah told the lifeguard.

"Sure you can," he said with a laugh.

SKILL PRACTICE Read the question. Fill in the bubble next to the correct answer.

1. **Which one is make-believe?**
   - Ⓐ A lifeguard saves a girl.
   - Ⓑ A lifeguard starts to worry.
   - Ⓒ A girl breathes underwater.
   - Ⓓ A girl swims across a pool.

2. **Which of these is make-believe?**
   - Ⓐ ships
   - Ⓑ whales
   - Ⓒ dolphins
   - Ⓓ mermaids

3. **Which one is real?**
   - Ⓐ Sarah saw sunken treasure.
   - Ⓑ Sarah is a fish.
   - Ⓒ Sarah can hold her breath underwater.
   - Ⓓ Sarah is a mermaid.

4. **Why does the lifeguard laugh?**
   - Ⓐ He does not believe Sarah.
   - Ⓑ He is not sure if Sarah is real.
   - Ⓒ He is glad that he saved Sarah.
   - Ⓓ He thinks that Sarah looks funny.

STRATEGY PRACTICE Tell a partner something you pictured when you read the passage.

READ THE PASSAGE   What happens to the main character that is fantasy?

The Flute

Once upon a time, there was a young man named Len. He was unhappy because he wasn't good at sports. Len's older brother was very good at shooting his bow and arrow. Len's younger brother could ride a horse very well. Len wanted to do something very well, too.

One day, Len took a walk in the woods. He heard some beautiful music. He followed the sound. But he could not tell where it was coming from.

Just then a woodpecker appeared. "The music is coming from this dry branch," it said. "I pecked the holes with my beak. The wind makes the music when it goes through the holes."

"I wish that I could make music like that," Len said. "Then I would be special."

"Break the branch from the tree and take it with you," said the woodpecker.

Len went home and played his new flute for everyone. The people in his town loved the music. His brothers clapped. Len felt happy.

SKILL PRACTICE   Read the question. Fill in the bubble next to the correct answer.

1. **Why does Len feel sad?**

   Ⓐ He has lost his bow and arrow.

   Ⓑ He is not good at sports.

   Ⓒ He wants his own horse.

   Ⓓ He cannot find the music.

2. **Which one is make-believe?**

   Ⓐ wind that blows

   Ⓑ brothers who clap

   Ⓒ a woodpecker that talks

   Ⓓ a boy who makes music

3. **How is Len different at the end of the story?**

   Ⓐ He does not care about sports.

   Ⓑ He has a woodpecker for a friend.

   Ⓒ He can ride a horse.

   Ⓓ He can do something well.

4. **Which one could be real?**

   Ⓐ A brother rides a horse.

   Ⓑ A tree plays a tune.

   Ⓒ A young man obeys a bird.

   Ⓓ A bird makes a flute.

STRATEGY PRACTICE   Write to tell something you do well or would like to do well.

_____

Author's Purpose
Students think about why an author wrote a particular passage.

Prediction
Students use clues from the text and their own background knowledge to anticipate what is likely to happen next or what information will come next.

DAY 1

Review the *Author's Purpose* skill with students. Say: **When we know why the author wrote what we are reading, it is easier to understand the main ideas of the passage or story.** Then remind students of the common reasons why authors write: to give information, to tell a story that entertains, to tell how to do something, or to persuade. Read the instructions at the top of the page aloud. Then have students read the passage. When students have finished, direct them to complete the skill practice activity. Review the answers together. For the strategy practice activity, remind students of the *Ask Questions* strategy, which was taught during Week 5. Say: **Asking questions about the information you've read will help you remember it.** Direct students to complete the strategy practice activity. Invite volunteers to share their responses.

DAY 2

Remind students of the *Author's Purpose* skill, and review the most common purposes (to give information, to entertain, to tell how to do something, and to persuade). Read the instructions at the top of the page aloud. Then remind students of the *Make Connections* strategy, which was taught during Week 1. Say: **As you read, think of what you know about puppies. This will help you understand what the author is saying.** Then direct students to read the passage and to complete the skill practice activity. For the strategy practice activity, pair students or complete it as a group.

DAY 3

Review the *Prediction* skill with students. Say: **When we predict, we use information from the passage and our own experiences to make a good guess about what is likely to happen next.** Hold a playground ball in front of you. Ask: **What will happen if I let go of the ball?** (It will fall and bounce.) **You know that will happen because you've seen it happen before. You used your experiences to make a prediction of what will happen next.** Tell students that they will read about what happens during a day at the beach. Remind students of the *Ask Questions* strategy. Say: **As you read, ask questions about what is happening and what might happen next.** Then read the instructions at the top of the page aloud. Direct students to read the passage and to complete the activities. Review the answers together, and invite volunteers to share their responses to the strategy practice activity.

DAY 4

Remind students of the *Prediction* skill and the *Make Connections* strategy. Then say: **Making connections is a good way to help you with making predictions. You can use your experiences of things you have done or seen that are like what you are reading about. You will read a story about children who are playing a game you've all played before, hide-and-seek. Having played that game will make it easy for you to make a connection to the story and to predict what will happen next.** Read the instructions at the top of the page aloud. Then direct students to read the passage and to complete the skill practice activity. Review the answers together. For the strategy practice activity, pair students or complete it as a group.

DAY 5

Tell students they will practice both the *Author's Purpose* and *Prediction* skills. Then remind them of the *Ask Questions* strategy. Read the instructions at the top of the page aloud. Then say: **You will also want to ask yourself questions about what might happen next.** Have students read the passage. When students have finished, direct them to complete the skill and strategy practice activities. Review the answers together.

READ THE PASSAGE   Ask yourself why the author wrote the passage.

Beach Cleanup Day

I went to the beach with my class today, but not to swim and play. We went to the beach to work. We wanted to do something nice for our town.

Our job was to pick up trash left on the sand. There are trash cans there, but some people do not use them. They leave soda cans, paper plates, and other kinds of trash right on the ground!

My teacher made cleaning up the beach a game. She put us in teams. She gave each team a big bag. The team that picked up the most trash would win a prize. I wondered what it would be.

Off we went! My friends and I ran around like ants in a picnic basket. Into the bags went lots of trash. The beach looked better and better. We all felt good about the work we did. We took a rest in the shade and ate a snack. We knew where to put our trash!

SKILL PRACTICE   Read the question. Fill in the bubble next to the correct answer.

1. **What would be another good title for the passage?**
   Ⓐ "Going to the Beach"
   Ⓑ "Team Games"
   Ⓒ "Acting Like Ants"
   Ⓓ "Kids Can Help"

2. **The author thinks that people should _____.**
   Ⓐ get prizes for helping
   Ⓑ clean up their messes
   Ⓒ leave their food at home
   Ⓓ stay away from beaches

3. **Why does the author mention ants?**
   Ⓐ to tell about a class picnic
   Ⓑ to show that bugs like trash
   Ⓒ to show that the kids move fast
   Ⓓ to tell about bugs that live in sand

4. **The author shows that kids can _____.**
   Ⓐ do helpful things
   Ⓑ win nice prizes
   Ⓒ run around like ants
   Ⓓ obey their teachers

STRATEGY PRACTICE   Write a question that can be answered by reading "Beach Cleanup Day."

_____

READ THE PASSAGE Look for things the author wants you to know.

Time for a Puppy?

Puppies are so soft and cute! They are fun to play with, too. But puppies are not easy to care for. It takes a lot of work to have a puppy.

A new puppy needs a lot of attention. It must have a safe place to be when you are not there. When you are with the puppy, you must watch it carefully. Puppies don't know about things that could hurt them.

You must give a puppy toys to chew, or it will chew your things. Keep your shoes, clothes, and library books off the floor. They look like good chew toys to a puppy. A puppy doesn't know what is a toy and what is not.

Puppies cost money to care for, too. They need food to eat. They need collars and leashes. They must see the vet to keep them healthy.

Puppies are very nice to have. But before you bring one home, make sure you are ready for it.

SKILL PRACTICE Read the question. Fill in the bubble next to the correct answer.

1. The author wrote the passage to _____.
   Ⓐ tell a fun story about puppies
   Ⓑ let you know that puppies need a lot of care
   Ⓒ help you choose the best kind of puppy
   Ⓓ stop people from getting puppies

2. Puppies need toys so they _____.
   Ⓐ will not chew the wrong things
   Ⓑ have something to sleep with
   Ⓒ can learn to share
   Ⓓ can be healthy

3. The author says to keep books off the floor because _____.
   Ⓐ the library would not like that
   Ⓑ it is hard to read on the floor
   Ⓒ a puppy might chew them
   Ⓓ you might trip on them

4. What does the author think people should do before they get puppies?
   Ⓐ take long walks alone
   Ⓑ read books about dogs
   Ⓒ get checked by a doctor
   Ⓓ make sure they are ready for a pet

STRATEGY PRACTICE Tell a partner what you know about taking care of a puppy.

READ THE PASSAGE Ask yourself what is likely to happen next.

Dark Cloud

Tito and Alma were on vacation at the seashore with their parents. They were playing in the water. The water was warm. There were no clouds in the sky.

All at once, huge dark clouds appeared. They rolled over the sun. The sky grew dark, and big, warm drops of rain began to fall.

"Out of the water!" the lifeguards shouted. "Everyone out! Right now!" Tito and Alma were very confused. They ran up to the snack building with their parents. They stood under the edge of the roof with the other people.

"It is not safe to be in the water during storms," someone said. "The lifeguards are protecting us from lightning." Soon the clouds were overhead. Heavy rain fell, and thunder rumbled loudly as the clouds passed by.

Moments later, the sun came back out. The storm was already over! Tito and Alma were amazed. They could not believe how fast the weather had changed.

SKILL PRACTICE Read the question. Fill in the bubble next to the correct answer.

1. **Why do you think the lifeguards shout?**
   - Ⓐ They want people to be safe.
   - Ⓑ They do not want people to get wet.
   - Ⓒ They do not like the people.
   - Ⓓ The people are not listening.

2. **What do you think surprises Tito and Alma?**
   - Ⓐ how fast the people run
   - Ⓑ how fast the storm passes
   - Ⓒ how warm the rain feels
   - Ⓓ how strong the lifeguards are

3. **What will the children probably do after the storm passes?**
   - Ⓐ go back into the water
   - Ⓑ stay near the building
   - Ⓒ ask the lifeguards for help
   - Ⓓ say they want to go home

4. **What will the people probably do if more dark clouds appear?**
   - Ⓐ run back into the water
   - Ⓑ stand under the snack building roof
   - Ⓒ yell at the lifeguards
   - Ⓓ wish for thunder and lightning

STRATEGY PRACTICE What is one question you asked as you read the passage?

_____

READ THE PASSAGE Think about what "It" should do next.

Hide-and-Seek

"Four, three, two, one. Ready or not, here I come!" Joni and her friends were playing hide-and-seek. Andy had found Joni hiding in the broom closet, so it was her turn to be *It.* The one who was *It* had to try to find the others who were hiding.

Joni walked into the den. It was very quiet. She thought she heard a giggle coming from nearby. She looked under the desk and behind the bookshelf. No one was hiding there, though. She tried the bathroom next.

Joni looked in the shower, but no one was hiding in there. Just as she was leaving the bathroom, she saw something blue behind the door. Max was wearing a blue shirt today. Could that be him? It was! "I found you! You're *It* now, Max," Joni said. Max laughed as he came out from his hiding place.

SKILL PRACTICE Read the question. Fill in the bubble next to the correct answer.

1. What might Joni do next?
   Ⓐ look for Max again
   Ⓑ look for Andy
   Ⓒ find a place to hide
   Ⓓ stop playing the game

2. If Joni sees something blue again, she might _____.
   Ⓐ think it is a blue towel
   Ⓑ think it is Max coming to look for her
   Ⓒ think it is Andy in the broom closet
   Ⓓ be *It* again

3. What do you think the other kids will do right after Joni finds Max?
   Ⓐ move to new hiding places
   Ⓑ tell Max to find a new hiding place
   Ⓒ wait for Joni to find a hiding place
   Ⓓ come out from their hiding places

4. What do you think Max will do when it is his turn to be *It?*
   Ⓐ wait for the others to hide
   Ⓑ look for a new place to hide
   Ⓒ tell Joni that the game is over
   Ⓓ ask Joni to help find the others

STRATEGY PRACTICE Tell a partner about your favorite game.

Daily Reading Comprehension • EMC 3452 • © Evan-Moor Corp.

READ THE PASSAGE Why do you think the author wrote the passage?

Old Toys

You have grown too tall for your clothes from last year. Your shoes are too small for your feet. You are also too old now for some of your toys. What will you do with them?

Don't just push old toys under the bed. No one can play with them there. You can give them to children who would enjoy the toys. You can give them to a children's hospital. Little girls and boys who are sick would enjoy playing with them.

Maybe you and your friends want to buy something new for yourselves. If so, you can gather all your old toys and have a big yard sale!

Ask a parent to help you. Make big signs that tell about your sale. Hang the signs around town. On the day of your sale, shoppers will come. Some will pay money for your old toys. Then you can have fun planning what new toys to buy.

SKILL PRACTICE Read the question. Fill in the bubble next to the correct answer.

1. The author thinks old toys should be _____.

   Ⓐ left in a backyard

   Ⓑ thrown in the trash

   Ⓒ made into new ones

   Ⓓ shared with other children

2. Which of these might the author say?

   Ⓐ "Old toys are worthless."

   Ⓑ "It is good to reuse things."

   Ⓒ "Keep your toys forever."

   Ⓓ "Do not buy any new toys."

3. What do you think the money from a yard sale will be spent on?

   Ⓐ new toys

   Ⓑ old shoes

   Ⓒ a big sign

   Ⓓ a trash can

4. What do you think will happen to the old toys in the passage?

   Ⓐ They will be left in a backyard.

   Ⓑ Parents will think they are trash.

   Ⓒ Younger kids will play with them.

   Ⓓ They will be pushed under a bed.

STRATEGY PRACTICE What is another thing you would want to know if you decided to have a yard sale?

_____

Nonfiction Text Features

Students look at text features, such as headings and captions, to better understand what they read.

Visual Information

Students discover how pictures, charts, graphs, and other visual elements can explain more about a topic.

DAY 1

Remind students that nonfiction text features are related to the main body of text in a passage but different from it. Show them features such as a table of contents, captions, headings, etc. Say: **It is important to pay attention to nonfiction text features because they help us understand what we are reading.** Then remind students of the *Determine Important Information* strategy, which was taught during Week 4. Tell students that looking for nonfiction text features can help to identify which information is most important. Then read the instructions at the top of the page aloud. Say: **You will be reading a class newsletter that was written to tell what is going on in class.** Read the newsletter aloud as a class, calling on individuals to read various sections, and pointing out the headlines as nonfiction text features. Direct students to complete the skill practice activity, and then review the answers together. Complete the strategy practice activity as a group, asking students to give reasons for their choices.

DAY 2

Remind students of the *Nonfiction Text Features* skill. Then remind them of the *Organization* strategy, which was taught during Week 3. Say: **Nonfiction text features can be organized in a way to make information easier to find.** Read the instructions at the top of the page aloud. Ask students to look at the flier and determine what kind of information it is (a lost pet flier). Read the flier aloud together, calling students' attention to the headings. Then discuss what kind of information they think will follow. Direct students to complete the skill practice activity, and review the answers together. For the strategy practice activity, pair students or complete it as a group.

DAY 3

Remind students that visual information can be given as pictures, graphs, charts, and maps, and that sometimes visual information is easier and quicker to understand than text. Tell students they are going to study an ad for pottery classes. Remind students of the *Determine Important Information* strategy and how they should not be distracted by interesting information that may not help them figure out what they need to know about the classes. Read the instructions at the top of the page aloud. Give students time to look at the ad. Tell students that this ad combines visual information with nonfiction text features. Then discuss what can be learned from the starburst and map (how to save $5; where the art center is located). Ask volunteers to read the words in the ad. Direct students to complete the skill practice activity independently. Review the answers together. Then direct students to complete the strategy practice activity and to share their responses. Help students to evaluate the importance of their choices.

DAY 4

Review that *visual information* is the term for non-word features such as pictures, maps, and graphs. Remind students of the *Organization* strategy. Then tell students that the chart shows the lunch menu for Sunshine School for one week. This may give them a clue as to how the information is organized. Give students time to study the chart. Then read it aloud together. Direct students to complete the skill practice activity, and review the answers together. Discuss the strategy practice activity as a group, writing a summary response on the board for students to copy.

DAY 5

Tell students they will practice both the *Nonfiction Text Features* and *Visual Information* skills. Remind students of the *Determine Important Information* strategy. Say: **Studying nonfiction text features and visual information will help you determine which information is important.** Tell students they will read a program for a school event. Guide students through the program. Then direct students to complete the activities independently. Review the answers together.

READ THE NEWSLETTER   Look for sentences that give the most important information.

CLASS NEWS

Monster Math
We have been learning our times-five facts. Be ready for the test this Friday.

Fall Spelling Tree
Our vowel trees are filling with leaves! Hang words with short vowels on the Short Vowel tree. Hang words with long vowels on the Long Vowel tree.

Creepy Crafts
We need more paper spiders and bats to hang in our classroom!

HALLOWEEN PARTY
OCTOBER 31
Wear a costume to school! Bring a healthy snack to share. Parent helpers are welcome.

Pumpkin Picking
The pumpkins in our school garden are ready to be picked. Be there Tuesday at lunchtime if you would like to pick one!

SKILL PRACTICE   Read the question. Fill in the bubble next to the correct answer.

1. The title tells that the news is mostly about _____.
   - Ⓐ an after-school club
   - Ⓑ a whole school
   - Ⓒ the parent–teacher group
   - Ⓓ one class in a school

2. The headings tell about _____.
   - Ⓐ what happens on one day
   - Ⓑ when a party will be
   - Ⓒ each news item
   - Ⓓ classroom decorations

3. What are the two news items on the right side of the newsletter about?
   - Ⓐ fun happenings
   - Ⓑ math tests
   - Ⓒ spelling trees
   - Ⓓ classroom needs

4. Which heading should parents pay attention to?
   - Ⓐ "Pumpkin Picking"
   - Ⓑ "Halloween Party"
   - Ⓒ "Monster Math"
   - Ⓓ "Fall Spelling Tree"

STRATEGY PRACTICE   Underline the information in the newsletter that tells about schoolwork.

READ THE FLIER   Notice the order in which the information is given.

MISSING CAT

We cannot find our cat!
We miss him very much.
Please help us!

HOW HE LOOKS

He is gray and white.
His front paws are white like boxing
gloves. His name is Boxer.

HOW HE SOUNDS

Boxer is big, but he cries like a kitten.
If you hear a tiny meow and see that it
is coming from a big, strong cat, then
you have found Boxer!

IF YOU SEE HIM

Please call 555-5555 or bring him
to our house at 10 Cherry Lane.
We will give you a reward.

SKILL PRACTICE   Read the question. Fill in the bubble next to the correct answer.

1. The title tells that someone _____.

   Ⓐ lost something

   Ⓑ wants to buy something

   Ⓒ found something

   Ⓓ wants to sell something

2. Which part would you read to know
   where to take Boxer?

   Ⓐ "If You See Him"

   Ⓑ "How He Looks"

   Ⓒ "Missing Cat"

   Ⓓ "How He Sounds"

3. What does the picture show?

   Ⓐ where Boxer lives

   Ⓑ how Boxer sounds

   Ⓒ what Boxer looks like

   Ⓓ who Boxer belongs to

4. The heading "If You See Him"
   tells _____.

   Ⓐ how Boxer got lost

   Ⓑ where to look for Boxer

   Ⓒ who is looking for Boxer

   Ⓓ what to do if you find Boxer

STRATEGY PRACTICE   With a partner, talk about how the capitalized headings help you
understand the information.

READ THE AD Look for important information about the pottery classes.

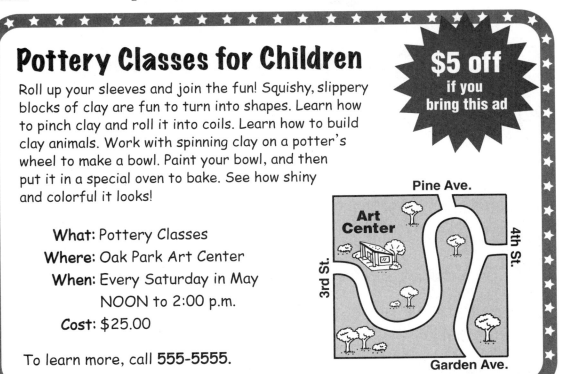

Pottery Classes for Children

Roll up your sleeves and join the fun! Squishy, slippery blocks of clay are fun to turn into shapes. Learn how to pinch clay and roll it into coils. Learn how to build clay animals. Work with spinning clay on a potter's wheel to make a bowl. Paint your bowl, and then put it in a special oven to bake. See how shiny and colorful it looks!

$5 off
if you
bring this ad

What: Pottery Classes
Where: Oak Park Art Center
When: Every Saturday in May
NOON to 2:00 p.m.
Cost: $25.00

To learn more, call **555-5555**.

SKILL PRACTICE Read the question. Fill in the bubble next to the correct answer.

1. One thing the title tells is _____.

   Ⓐ who the classes are for

   Ⓑ when the classes will be

   Ⓒ where the classes will be

   Ⓓ how much the classes cost

2. The headings tell important information about _____.

   Ⓐ Oak Park

   Ⓑ a potter's wheel

   Ⓒ the pottery classes

   Ⓓ a paint called glaze

3. What do you learn in the starburst?

   Ⓐ who the pottery teacher is

   Ⓑ what to wear to the class

   Ⓒ how to sign up for the class

   Ⓓ how to pay less for the class

4. The best way to reach Oak Park Art Center is to use the entrance on _____.

   Ⓐ Pine Ave.

   Ⓑ 3rd St.

   Ⓒ 4th St.

   Ⓓ Garden Ave.

STRATEGY PRACTICE Circle three important things you need to know if you want to take a pottery class.

READ THE MENU Read the information on the menu carefully.

Sunshine School Lunch Menu
March 5 – March 9

Monday
Tacos
Refried Beans
Green Salad
Lemonade

Tuesday
Chicken Sandwich
Fruit Salad
Yogurt and Berries
Orange Juice

Wednesday
Chili
Cheese Cubes
Cornbread
Apple Cider

Thursday
Turkey Corn Dogs
Potato Wedges
Sliced Apples
Lemonade or Milk

Friday
Pizza
Veggies and Dip
Oatmeal Cookies
Grape Juice

SKILL PRACTICE Read the question. Fill in the bubble next to the correct answer.

1. What does the menu show?
   Ⓐ meals at a school
   Ⓑ foods from a garden
   Ⓒ meals kids will cook
   Ⓓ foods kids will shop for

2. The menu tells about one school _____.
   Ⓐ day
   Ⓑ year
   Ⓒ week
   Ⓓ month

3. The drink on Monday is _____.
   Ⓐ milk
   Ⓑ lemonade
   Ⓒ grape juice
   Ⓓ apple cider

4. On which day are corn dogs served?
   Ⓐ Friday
   Ⓑ Monday
   Ⓒ Tuesday
   Ⓓ Thursday

STRATEGY PRACTICE How is the menu organized to help you understand the information?

_____

READ THE PROGRAM Notice the features that help you understand the information.

SKILL PRACTICE Read the question. Fill in the bubble next to the correct answer.

1. **What do the pictures show?**

   Ⓐ when the play will be

   Ⓑ where the play will be

   Ⓒ who will be in the play

   Ⓓ who will watch the play

2. **Who plays Town Mouse?**

   Ⓐ Sharon

   Ⓑ Raymond

   Ⓒ Jill

   Ⓓ Roberto

3. **Under the "Scene" headings, you can read about _____.**

   Ⓐ who is in the play

   Ⓑ when the play happens

   Ⓒ what the play is about

   Ⓓ where the play takes place

4. **The name of the play is a heading for _____.**

   Ⓐ the reason for the play

   Ⓑ what the play is about

   Ⓒ who the plays are shown for

   Ⓓ where the costumes are from

STRATEGY PRACTICE Why do you think pictures of the actors are included?

_____

Main Idea and Details

Students look for the central idea or message of a passage or story. They also find details that best support the main idea.

Sequence

Students look for the order of events or steps in a process.

DAY 1

Review the *Main Idea and Details* skill with students. Say: **Remember that the *main idea* is what a passage is mostly about. Ideas that tell us more about the main idea are called *details*.** Read the instructions at the top of the page aloud. Say: **As good readers, we stop while reading and ask, *What is the most important idea of the part I just read?* When we do this, we practice the *Monitor Comprehension* strategy** (taught during Week 6). Have students read the passage. Then direct students to complete the skill practice activity, and review the answers together. For the strategy practice activity, pair students or complete it as a group.

DAY 2

Remind students of the *Main Idea and Details* skill, and then read the instructions at the top of the page aloud. Tell students they are going to be reading about wagon trains—a way pioneers traveled across the United States long ago, before automobiles were invented. Remind students of the *Determine Important Information* strategy (taught during Week 4). Say: **It's important to notice which details tell important things.** Call on volunteers to read the passage aloud. Stop after each paragraph to clarify information that may be new to students. Determine as a group the main idea of each paragraph. Record the main ideas on the board. Direct students to complete the skill practice activity independently. Review the answers together. For the strategy practice activity, pair students or complete it as a group.

DAY 3

Ask students to recall the name of the skill good readers are using when they pay attention to the order in which events happen (*Sequence*). Say: **We are going to read about a girl who visits her aunt. Remembering the sequence in which things happen will help you to understand the story. Good readers stop while reading to monitor their comprehension. They ask themselves if they remember the sequence of events.** Direct students to read the passage and to complete the skill practice activity. Review the answers together. Pair students to complete the strategy practice activity, reminding them to listen to make sure their partners tell the information in the correct sequence.

DAY 4

Write the words *First, Next, Then,* and *Last* on the board. Remind students of the *Sequence* skill. Say: **Writers often use certain words to help the reader understand the sequence in which things are happening. We call these words *signal words*. Let's read the signal words on the board together.** Read the instructions at the top of the page and the title aloud. Then say: **You are going to read about how chocolate candy is made. Passages that tell the steps in a process often use signal words so that the order of doing things is clear to the reader. Signal words help the reader to practice the *Determine Important Information* strategy.** Remind students to notice signal words as they read the passage. Then direct students to read the passage and to complete the skill practice activity. Review the answers together. Complete the strategy practice activity as a group. Reread paragraph 2 aloud and allow students to suggest important ideas. Then guide the group to decide on the four most important ideas in the paragraph and number them.

DAY 5

Tell students they will practice both the *Main Idea and Details* and *Sequence* skills as they read about taking care of their teeth. Read the instructions at the top of the page aloud. Remind students to use the *Monitor Comprehension* strategy to help them find the three things. Then direct students to read the passage and to complete the activities. Review the answers together.

READ THE PASSAGE Tell yourself what each paragraph is about.

How Do They Do That?

They swing, they jump, they tumble, and they flip. Acrobats can do amazing things! Their acts are thrilling to watch.

Music plays as men climb onto each other's shoulders. They build a tower of people. The man at the top stands on his hands. Then he juggles three balls with his feet!

A woman swings from a bar that hangs from the top of the tent. She lets go of the bar and flips three times in the air. Then she lands in a big net below.

A man rides a bike across a wire near the top of the tent. He goes forward and then backward. He balances in one spot. The people in the crowd hold their breath until he reaches the other side.

"Hooray!" the crowd shouts. "He made it!" The people clap their hands. Then they wait for another daring act to begin.

SKILL PRACTICE Read the question. Fill in the bubble next to the correct answer.

1. **What is the passage about?**
   - Ⓐ people holding their breath
   - Ⓑ performers doing hard tricks
   - Ⓒ men climbing to music
   - Ⓓ a man riding a bike

2. **The man at the top of the tower _____.**
   - Ⓐ claps his hands
   - Ⓑ shouts "Hooray!"
   - Ⓒ flips high in the air
   - Ⓓ juggles some balls

3. **The woman acrobat _____.**
   - Ⓐ does flips and lands in a net
   - Ⓑ swings and waves to the crowd
   - Ⓒ stays at the top of the tent
   - Ⓓ throws balls to the bike rider

4. **The crowd waits for _____.**
   - Ⓐ the music to play
   - Ⓑ a turn to ride the bike
   - Ⓒ the next act to begin
   - Ⓓ a chance to jump into the net

STRATEGY PRACTICE Discuss with a partner which of the acts described in the passage seemed the most difficult. Why?

READ THE PASSAGE Tell yourself what each paragraph is about.

Wagon Train

Long ago, before cars and airplanes, it was not easy for people to move across the country. They found a way to do it, but the trip was long and hard. They put their belongings into wagons. They packed tables, chairs, beds, and blankets. They packed food and water, too. The wagons were covered by tents. They were pulled by horses, oxen, or mules. Some people rode in the wagons. Others walked beside their wagons. Many wagons went together in a long line.

The wagons moved slowly across the land. The trail was dusty and bumpy. Sometimes the weather was hot. Sometimes it was cold and snowy. The people became very tired. They wondered if they would ever get to a new home.

Every day when the sun went down, they stopped to rest. They gave water to the animals. They formed a circle with their wagons and built a campfire in the middle. They cooked their dinners and told stories near the fire. Then they went to sleep under the starry sky.

SKILL PRACTICE Read the question. Fill in the bubble next to the correct answer.

1. The passage is about people who _____.

   Ⓐ sleep outside

   Ⓑ have animals

   Ⓒ move to a new place

   Ⓓ become tired

2. How do the people travel?

   Ⓐ in tents

   Ⓑ on trains

   Ⓒ on mules

   Ⓓ in wagons

3. Which of these things did people not bring on their trip?

   Ⓐ food

   Ⓑ sleds

   Ⓒ beds

   Ⓓ animals

4. What do the people do when it gets dark?

   Ⓐ stop to rest

   Ⓑ ride in the wagons

   Ⓒ cook dinner for the animals

   Ⓓ make circles on the ground

STRATEGY PRACTICE Think of a sentence that tells the main idea of each paragraph. Then share your sentence with a partner.

READ THE PASSAGE Remember the order in which Maria experiences things.

A Visit

Maria stepped out of her mother's car. She took a deep breath. The cool mountain air smelled like pine trees. "Welcome!" said Auntie Ann as she hugged Maria and her mother. Auntie Ann smelled like lemon soap.

The cozy kitchen smelled good, too. "You are just in time to help with dinner," Auntie Ann said. "There is a turkey in the oven. Will you put some cinnamon on the sweet potatoes?"

After dinner, it was time for a bath. Maria's aunt poured some powder into the tub. The water turned blue. The steamy bathroom filled with the smell of flowers. "Ahh," sighed Maria as she sank into the warm, sudsy water.

"Sleep well," said Auntie Ann as she kissed Maria good night. "Tomorrow we will go to the lake." Maria smiled. Her pillow smelled like fresh mountain air.

"Good night, Auntie Ann," said Maria. "I love staying with you. Your life smells so good!"

SKILL PRACTICE Read the question. Fill in the bubble next to the correct answer.

1. **What does Maria smell first?**
   - Ⓐ trees
   - Ⓑ soap
   - Ⓒ turkey
   - Ⓓ flowers

2. **Which of these does Maria do first?**
   - Ⓐ take a bath
   - Ⓑ hug her aunt
   - Ⓒ go to the lake
   - Ⓓ help with dinner

3. **After her bath, Maria _____.**
   - Ⓐ eats dinner
   - Ⓑ picks flowers
   - Ⓒ goes to bed
   - Ⓓ makes lemon pie

4. **When does Maria smell turkey?**
   - Ⓐ as she gets into bed
   - Ⓑ as she gets into the tub
   - Ⓒ after she goes to the lake
   - Ⓓ after she goes into the kitchen

STRATEGY PRACTICE Tell a partner how Maria spends time when she visits her aunt.

READ THE PASSAGE   Look for steps in making chocolate bars.

Chocolate

Chocolate candy bars are a rich and sweet treat. Have you ever wondered where chocolate comes from and how candy bars are made?

Chocolate starts as cocoa beans. Cocoa beans grow in football-shaped pods on cocoa trees. These trees grow where the weather is warm and wet. First, the pods are cut from the trees. Next, the pods are split open, and the beans are removed. Then, the beans are spread out in the sun to dry. You would not want to eat these cocoa beans yet. They taste bitter, not sweet.

After the beans are dry, they are shipped all over the world. Candy makers cook the beans in big ovens. They use machines to remove the bean shells. Then, they mash the beans into a paste. The paste is heated with sugar, vanilla, milk, and other things. The chocolate is mixed until it is smooth.

Last, the chocolate is poured into molds that shape it into bars. Then, the bars are wrapped. One is ready for you!

SKILL PRACTICE   Read the question. Fill in the bubble next to the correct answer.

1. Which one happens first?
   Ⓐ Cocoa pods are split open.
   Ⓑ Cocoa beans are shipped.
   Ⓒ Cocoa pods are cut from trees.
   Ⓓ Cocoa beans are mashed into a paste.

2. The beans are shipped after they are _____.
   Ⓐ dried in the sun
   Ⓑ baked in an oven
   Ⓒ mixed with sugar
   Ⓓ poured into molds

3. Which of these is the last step?
   Ⓐ The paste is heated.
   Ⓑ The bars are wrapped.
   Ⓒ The shells are removed.
   Ⓓ The chocolate is cooled.

4. What do candy makers do right after they get the beans?
   Ⓐ dry them
   Ⓑ cool them
   Ⓒ pour them
   Ⓓ cook them

STRATEGY PRACTICE   Number four important ideas about cocoa beans in paragraph 2.

READ THE PASSAGE   Look for three things the writer thinks you should do.

Taking Care of Your Teeth

Your teeth are important. Think of all the things you could not eat without them. To have strong teeth all your life, you need to take good care of them.

Caring for teeth starts with eating healthy food. Think about what you eat. Sticky candy and sweet soda hurt your teeth. The sugar in them sticks to your teeth. If it is left there, little holes can form in the teeth.

You should brush your teeth after every meal. Don't rush! It takes about two minutes to do a good job. Next, use floss to remove food between the teeth that a toothbrush cannot reach.

Dentists have tools that clean teeth better than you can at home. And they have special cameras to take pictures of your teeth. If your teeth are hurting, a dentist can fix them.

So, take good care of your teeth at home, and visit the dentist every year. Then you'll be able to keep on eating all that chewy, crunchy, healthy food.

SKILL PRACTICE   Read the question. Fill in the bubble next to the correct answer.

1. What is the passage about?
   Ⓐ where to find a dentist
   Ⓑ how to care for your teeth
   Ⓒ where to buy healthy food
   Ⓓ how to take pictures of teeth

2. Dentists fill holes in teeth to _____.
   Ⓐ make chewing easier
   Ⓑ make teeth look shinier
   Ⓒ keep the holes from getting bigger
   Ⓓ keep floss from sticking to them

3. What does the writer say you should do first?
   Ⓐ Floss between your teeth.
   Ⓑ Brush your teeth well.
   Ⓒ Have your picture taken.
   Ⓓ Think about what you eat.

4. What should you do after you brush?
   Ⓐ Floss between your teeth.
   Ⓑ Go see the dentist.
   Ⓒ Eat a piece of candy.
   Ⓓ Take a picture of your teeth.

STRATEGY PRACTICE   What is one important thing you learned about caring for your teeth?

Cause and Effect

Students practice the skill by looking for what happens (the effect) and why it happens (the cause).

Fact and Opinion

Students determine whether parts of the passage can be proved (facts) or represent what someone thinks or feels (opinions).

DAY 1

Review the *Cause and Effect* skill with students. Say: **When something happens, it is the effect. The reason why it happens is the cause. Sometimes the cause and the effect will be in the same sentence. Sometimes you will have to read further on in the passage to find the cause. It is important to read slowly and carefully to notice both the cause and its effect.** Read the instructions at the top of the page aloud. Then remind students of the *Visualization* strategy, which was taught during Week 2. Tell students that making a mental image of what happens is a good way to picture the causes and effects in a passage. Have students read the passage. When students have finished, direct them to complete the skill and strategy practice activities. Review the answers together, allowing volunteers to share the part of the story that created a vivid mental picture for them.

DAY 2

Remind students of the *Cause and Effect* skill and the *Organization* strategy, which was taught during Week 3. Inform students that writers may organize their stories to have several causes and several effects, and that good readers pay attention to things that happen and the reasons they happen. Read the instructions at the top of the page aloud. Then have students read the passage. When students have finished, direct them to complete the skill and strategy practice activities. Then review the answers together.

DAY 3

Review the *Fact and Opinion* skill with students. Say: **A fact can be proved. An opinion is what someone thinks or believes. If I tell you that horses have hooves, is that a fact or an opinion?** (fact) **If I tell you that horses are the most beautiful animals in the world, is that a fact or an opinion?** (opinion) **It's an opinion because it is only what I think. You may think something different.** Read the instructions at the top of the page aloud. Then remind students to use the *Visualization* strategy as a way to help them make mental images about what they have read. Direct students to read the passage and to complete the skill practice activity. Review the answers together. For the strategy practice activity, pair students or complete it as a group.

DAY 4

Remind students of the *Fact and Opinion* skill and the *Organization* strategy. Say: **One way writers make a passage interesting is to mix facts and opinions together. Just because you read a sentence that is a fact, you can't know that the next sentence will also be a fact. Writers may also give facts and opinions about one thing first and then give facts and opinions about another thing. Good readers ask,** *Is this a fact or an opinion? What is the fact or opinion about?* Read the instructions at the top of the page aloud. Direct students to read the passage and to complete the skill and strategy practice activities. Then review the answers together. For the strategy practice activity, point out to students that the writer organized the passage to describe each game in its own paragraph.

DAY 5

Tell students they will practice both the *Cause and Effect* and *Fact and Opinion* skills. Tell them they are going to read about a child's experience on a vacation. Say: **You will need to read carefully to find different cause-and-effect relationships, as well as examples of facts and opinions.** Then remind students that using the *Visualization* strategy can help them notice the causes, effects, facts, and opinions in a passage. Have students read the passage. When students have finished, direct them to complete the skill practice activity. Then review the answers together. For the strategy practice activity, pair students or complete it as a group.

READ THE PASSAGE Find out what makes Pete chubby.

Chubby Pup

My parents and I were worried about our little dog, Pete. He did not want to play anymore. He did not want to chase the ball. Pete was too tired. He just wanted to sleep. We took him to the pet doctor.

As the doctor checked him, Pete wagged his tail. Then he curled up to take a nap. "Pete is just fat!" the doctor said. "Are you giving him too much food?"

"No," we answered. "We are feeding him good dog food twice a day."

The doctor did not know what was wrong. "Try this special dog food," she said. We took Pete home and tried the new food, but he just grew fatter.

One day, I was picking up fruit that had fallen from our avocado tree. Some of the avocados looked strange. The dark, green peels had been ripped open. Part of the inside of each fruit was gone. I knew how Pete had gotten fat! I laughed out loud. Then I ran to tell my parents the good news.

SKILL PRACTICE Read the question. Fill in the bubble next to the correct answer.

1. Why are Pete's owners worried?
   Ⓐ Pete will not eat.
   Ⓑ Pete will not play.
   Ⓒ Pete is not growing.
   Ⓓ Pete is not sleeping.

2. The doctor says to try special dog food because _____.
   Ⓐ she thinks Pete will like it
   Ⓑ Pete is not eating good food
   Ⓒ she wants Pete to eat once a day
   Ⓓ she thinks it might help Pete lose weight

3. Pete's owner knows what happened when he sees _____.
   Ⓐ Pete eating avocados
   Ⓑ Pete sleeping under the tree
   Ⓒ avocados that have been eaten
   Ⓓ holes in the avocado tree

4. Pete grew fat from _____.
   Ⓐ eating too many avocados
   Ⓑ sleeping too much
   Ⓒ eating too much dog food
   Ⓓ not chasing the ball

STRATEGY PRACTICE Underline the part of the passage that made a strong picture in your mind.

READ THE PASSAGE Find out what makes a hot-air balloon go up and come down.

Up, Up, and Away!

It is still dark outside when you climb into the basket. "Sit down and hold on to the handles in front of you," says the pilot. A hot flame roars out of the burner in the basket. It heats the air inside the colorful balloon above you. A moment later, the pilot says you can stand up. Wow! You are high above the ground. You didn't even feel the balloon lift off!

You drift in silence. The only noise is when the pilot opens the burner. The burner keeps the balloon flying at the right height. You don't feel the wind at all. The pilot points out things on the ground. He explains how the balloon works.

When it's time to land, the pilot turns down the flame. The air inside the balloon cools. The balloon slowly sinks toward the ground. The pilot tells you how to get ready for the landing. With a soft bump, you are on the ground. A ride in a hot-air balloon is an exciting thing to do!

SKILL PRACTICE Read the question. Fill in the bubble next to the correct answer.

1. A hot-air balloon goes up when _____.
   Ⓐ there are enough people in the basket
   Ⓑ the air inside it is cooled
   Ⓒ the pilot tells people to sit down
   Ⓓ the air inside it is heated

2. Why do people ride in hot-air balloons?
   Ⓐ to help the pilot
   Ⓑ to have fun
   Ⓒ to keep the balloon cool
   Ⓓ to get back to their homes

3. What makes a balloon rise or sink?
   Ⓐ the handles in the basket
   Ⓑ the color of the balloon
   Ⓒ the flame in the burner
   Ⓓ the time of day

4. The pilot wants people to be safe, so he _____.
   Ⓐ tells them how to get ready to land
   Ⓑ tells them what is on the ground
   Ⓒ explains how the balloon works
   Ⓓ opens the burner

STRATEGY PRACTICE Draw a star next to the paragraph that tells about the wind.

READ THE PASSAGE Look for facts and opinions about raccoons.

Masked Pests

Raccoons are cute and furry. They have long whiskers and pointed ears like cats. Their bodies look heavy for their short legs. Their long, striped tails are very bushy. A raccoon's nose is narrow and pointed. See the rings around the raccoon's eyes? They look like a little dark mask.

Raccoons may be cute, but they can be pests. They sleep during the day, and come out at night to find food. Some raccoons live in the woods near ponds and streams. But many raccoons have learned to live around people. In the woods, raccoons eat fruit, nuts, insects, fish, and frogs. In towns, they eat people's trash.

A raccoon's front paws are a lot like our hands. These handy paws can do many clever things. They take the lids off garbage cans. They open jars, doors, and even locks!

When people see raccoons eating their trash, they try to shoo the raccoons away. The pesky raccoons do not run away, though. They are not afraid. They just keep eating the trash.

SKILL PRACTICE Read the question. Fill in the bubble next to the correct answer.

1. The writer thinks raccoons are _____.

  Ⓐ cute

  Ⓑ scary

  Ⓒ playful

  Ⓓ helpless

2. The writer thinks a raccoon's front paws _____.

  Ⓐ look fancy

  Ⓑ move slowly

  Ⓒ can do clever things

  Ⓓ work best at night

3. It is a fact that raccoons _____.

  Ⓐ are really cute animals

  Ⓑ have rings around their eyes

  Ⓒ wear a mask

  Ⓓ are the most clever animals

4. Which one is an opinion?

  Ⓐ Raccoons live in towns.

  Ⓑ Raccoons have long tails.

  Ⓒ Raccoons have whiskers.

  Ⓓ Raccoons are pesky.

STRATEGY PRACTICE Tell a partner what a raccoon looks like.

READ THE PASSAGE Notice which ideas are facts and which are opinions.

Parachute Play

My class played the best game ever today! Our teacher said there was a surprise for us out on the baseball field. When recess started, we ran out to see. Wow! A great big parachute was spread out on the grass. It was round and blue.

My classmates and I stood around the parachute. We each held a part of the edge. We lifted the chute up high in the air. It felt light! It puffed up with air. It looked beautiful! Our teacher tossed a beach ball onto the parachute. We made waves with the parachute and laughed as the beach ball bounced around.

Next, we played a game of tag. We lifted the parachute up over our heads. Then our teacher called out two names. The people whose names she called had to run under the parachute. They had to switch places with each other before the parachute sank. It was so much fun! I hope we can play again tomorrow.

SKILL PRACTICE Read the question. Fill in the bubble next to the correct answer.

1. The writer thinks the teacher's surprise is _____.
   Ⓐ sad
   Ⓑ magic
   Ⓒ wonderful
   Ⓓ confusing

2. The writer thinks the parachute is _____.
   Ⓐ heavy to lift
   Ⓑ easy to hide
   Ⓒ hard to share
   Ⓓ fun to play with

3. Which one is a fact?
   Ⓐ The class plays games.
   Ⓑ The parachute looks pretty.
   Ⓒ The teacher is nicer than others.
   Ⓓ The games are better than others.

4. Which word makes the sentence an opinion?
   The parachute is _____.
   Ⓐ big
   Ⓑ fun
   Ⓒ blue
   Ⓓ round

STRATEGY PRACTICE What two games did the class play with the parachute?

_____

READ THE PASSAGE Look for reasons things happen. Notice facts and opinions.

Old Faithful

"Why are all those people standing around looking at nothing?" I asked. We had just arrived at Yellowstone National Park. It took three boring days in the car to get here. So far, I hadn't seen anything very exciting.

Suddenly—*Whoosh!* A giant spray of water and steam shot high into the air. "Wow!" I guess that was what everyone was waiting for. Watching Old Faithful erupt is a pretty cool sight!

Old Faithful is a geyser (GUY-zer). Geysers can happen where hot, melted rock is not far under Earth's surface. The heat can make underground water boil. Pressure builds up until the water and steam shoot out suddenly.

Old Faithful was named by explorers in the 1800s. They noticed that the geyser erupted every 30 minutes to two hours. So far, the geyser is still faithful.

SKILL PRACTICE Read the question. Fill in the bubble next to the correct answer.

1. The geyser was named Old Faithful because _____.
   Ⓐ it is the oldest one in the park
   Ⓑ it was named a long time ago
   Ⓒ it always erupts after the same amount of time passes
   Ⓓ it erupts when you ask it to

2. Geysers are caused by _____.
   Ⓐ water under pressure
   Ⓑ big holes in the earth
   Ⓒ national park visitors
   Ⓓ water shooting in the air

3. It is a fact that Old Faithful is _____.
   Ⓐ the best thing in Yellowstone
   Ⓑ worth waiting for
   Ⓒ a cool thing to see
   Ⓓ a geyser

4. Which of these is an opinion?
   Ⓐ Geysers shoot out water and steam.
   Ⓑ The car trip was boring.
   Ⓒ People watch Old Faithful erupt.
   Ⓓ The geyser was named by explorers.

STRATEGY PRACTICE Tell a partner how you pictured Old Faithful.

Compare and Contrast
Students look for similarities and differences between two or more people or things.

Make Inferences
Students look for clues in the passage and draw upon their own experience to understand information that is not directly stated.

DAY 1

Review the *Compare and Contrast* skill with students. Say: **When we compare and contrast two or more things, we look for how they are alike and different.** Select two objects in the classroom—a pencil and a crayon, for example—and have students compare and contrast them. Read the instructions at the top of the page aloud. Then remind students of the *Ask Questions* strategy, which was taught during Week 5. Say: **As you read the passage, remember questions you have that the text does not answer.** Have students read the passage. When students have finished, make a list of questions that they generated during reading. Direct students to complete the strategy practice activity by copying one of the questions on the line provided. Then direct students to complete the skill practice activity. Review the answers together.

DAY 2

Remind students of the *Compare and Contrast* skill. Read the instructions at the top of the page aloud. Then remind students of the *Monitor Comprehension* strategy, which was taught during Week 6. Draw a Venn diagram on the board and tell students that using a diagram is a good way to keep track of how two things are the same or different. Read the passage aloud together. Stop after each paragraph to record information. After completing the Venn diagram, direct students to complete the skill practice activity independently, using the diagram to confirm answers. Review the answers together. For the strategy practice activity, pair students or complete it as a group.

DAY 3

Review the *Make Inferences* skill with students. Say: **When we make an inference, we use clues from the passage and our own experience to figure out information that we haven't been told.** Then say: **Imagine you leave your lunch on a picnic table at the park while you play on the swings. When you come back, some of your sandwich is missing. Then a squirrel scurries out from under the table. What do you suppose happened?** (squirrel ate the sandwich) **How do you know?** (bite out of sandwich; squirrel nearby) Read the instructions at the top of the page aloud. Remind students of the *Ask Questions* strategy. Tell them that asking questions about what they have just read will help them remember and understand the passage. Then direct students to read the passage and to complete the skill practice activity. Review the answers together. For the strategy practice activity, give students time to write their questions individually, and then pair students to question a partner.

DAY 4

Remind students of the *Make Inferences* skill. Tell students that frequently a passage will give facts they can use as clues to arrive at an inference about the topic. Then remind students of the *Monitor Comprehension* strategy and that as they read, they should pause to make sure they are understanding what fruits and flowers have to do with clothes. If they don't remember, they should reread. Read the instructions at the top of the page aloud. Direct students to read the passage and to complete the skill practice activity. Review the answers together. Complete the strategy practice activity as a group, locating all six color words (*orange, red, tan, pink, purple, green*) and deciding together which plants are used for each color. Record the information on the board and allow students to use the information to complete the strategy practice activity.

DAY 5

Tell students they will practice both the *Compare and Contrast* and *Make Inferences* skills. Remind students of the *Ask Questions* strategy—that one way to find out if you understood what you read is to think of questions to ask about the information. Read the instructions at the top of the page aloud. Direct students to read the passage and to complete the skill practice activity. Review the answers together. For the strategy practice activity, give students time to write their questions individually, and then pair students to question a partner.

READ THE PASSAGE How are the jobs alike and how are they different?

Working Outside

There are many different jobs in the world. Lots of jobs are in certain places outdoors. Tree trimmers and bridge builders do their work high in the air. People who take pictures of whales and sharks do their work at sea.

Some people work on ladders. They paint houses or they wash windows. Others mow grass in parks and on playing fields. They work outside on sunny days. Some lifeguards work on beaches. They watch children splash and play, and help to keep them safe.

Some animal doctors drive from farm to farm. They take care of horses and cows. Traffic police work on busy city streets. They blow their whistles. They wave their arms to direct drivers.

There are lots of outdoor places to work. Which one would you like best?

SKILL PRACTICE Read the question. Fill in the bubble next to the correct answer.

1. All the people in the passage _____.
   - Ⓐ climb ladders
   - Ⓑ work outside
   - Ⓒ work in parks
   - Ⓓ work with children

2. House painters and window washers both use _____.
   - Ⓐ lawn mowers
   - Ⓑ cameras
   - Ⓒ whistles
   - Ⓓ ladders

3. Lifeguards and _____ work near or in water.
   - Ⓐ tree trimmers
   - Ⓑ animal doctors
   - Ⓒ people who take pictures of whales
   - Ⓓ traffic police

4. How are some animal doctors different from the other workers?
   - Ⓐ They do their work on farms.
   - Ⓑ They travel on horses.
   - Ⓒ They keep children safe.
   - Ⓓ They drive on city streets.

STRATEGY PRACTICE What is something you would like to know about one of the jobs in the passage?

_____

READ THE PASSAGE What is the same and different about a bath and a shower?

Before Bedtime

Before I go to bed tonight, I might take a warm bath. Or maybe I should take a shower. Both sound very nice.

If I choose to take a bath, I'll add bubbles to the water. The room will fill with steam. The steam will smell like flowers. I'll make a silly bubble hat for my head. I'll wear a soap bubble beard. I'll soak in the tub for a long time. The bath will make me feel sleepy.

A shower would make me feel sleepy, too. It takes less time than a bath. I like to rub shampoo on my head and then rinse it off under the warm rain. I like to sing songs in the steamy shower. I like to use my mother's special soap. It makes me smell like lemons.

After my bath or shower, I'll put on my pajamas. Then I'll dream sweet dreams.

SKILL PRACTICE Read the question. Fill in the bubble next to the correct answer.

1. Baths and showers both make the writer _____.
   - Ⓐ feel like being silly
   - Ⓑ feel sleepy
   - Ⓒ smell like flowers
   - Ⓓ smell like a lemon

2. What does the writer do in showers that she does <u>not</u> do in baths?
   - Ⓐ sing songs
   - Ⓑ make silly hats
   - Ⓒ stay in a long time
   - Ⓓ add bubble soap

3. Baths and showers both make _____.
   - Ⓐ a warm rain
   - Ⓑ a flowery smell
   - Ⓒ steam in the room
   - Ⓓ bubbles in the water

4. The writer says that baths _____ than showers.
   - Ⓐ are cleaner
   - Ⓑ feel warmer
   - Ⓒ are more fun
   - Ⓓ take more time

STRATEGY PRACTICE With a partner, talk about what the writer says is nice about a bath and what is nice about a shower. Decide which one the writer should choose.

READ THE PASSAGE Think about how you would describe Jessica to someone.

Jessica Cox

Think of all the ways that you use your arms and hands. You use them to open doors and carry boxes. You use them to climb trees and ride bikes.

Jessica Cox was born without arms. But she didn't let that stop her from doing things. She learned to feed herself. She learned to paint and to play the piano. She uses her feet to do the things that most of us do with our hands.

When she was in school, Jessica watched the other children on the playground. She did not have hands to catch balls with. She did not have arms to climb with. Jessica imagined having superpowers. She would fly over the playground and take her friends for rides.

When Jessica grew up, she did fly. She learned to fly an airplane! It was hard work. She uses her feet to work the controls. Jessica is determined and brave. She made her dreams come true.

SKILL PRACTICE Read the question. Fill in the bubble next to the correct answer.

1. **Which of these do you think would be easiest for Jessica to do?**
   - Ⓐ climb a tree
   - Ⓑ play tennis
   - Ⓒ read a book
   - Ⓓ put books on a high shelf

2. **Which of these is probably true?**
   - Ⓐ Jessica does not drive a car.
   - Ⓑ Jessica will want to be an astronaut.
   - Ⓒ Jessica does not use a computer.
   - Ⓓ Jessica's toes work like fingers.

3. **Which of these might Jessica say?**
   - Ⓐ "If something is hard, do not do it."
   - Ⓑ "You can do anything you set your mind to."
   - Ⓒ "Learning new things is scary."
   - Ⓓ "I do not like to be challenged."

4. **Jessica Cox is a person who probably _____.**
   - Ⓐ is afraid to try things
   - Ⓑ has a hard time learning
   - Ⓒ does not give up easily
   - Ⓓ only daydreams of doing things

STRATEGY PRACTICE Write a question that can be answered by the passage. Have a partner answer your question.

READ THE PASSAGE Find out what flowers and fruits have to do with clothes.

Colorful Clothes

Look at all the bright, colorful clothes we wear! People started coloring, or dying, cloth hundreds of years ago. They used colors from nature. They used roots, nuts, bark, berries, and flowers to make colors.

First, they boiled water over a fire. Next, they chopped up parts of plants and added them to the water. In another pot, they soaked cloth in salty water. Then, they added the cloth to the colored water. When they pulled out the cloth, it was the color of the water.

To dye a piece of cloth orange, people used carrots or butternut squash. To dye cloth red, they used certain flowers or raspberries. They used walnuts or tree bark to turn cloth tan. They used strawberries for pink and grapes for purple. Plant leaves dyed cloth green.

Nature gives us so many beautiful colors. Which colors do you like to wear?

SKILL PRACTICE Read the question. Fill in the bubble next to the correct answer.

1. Even long ago, people wanted their clothes to be _____.
   - Ⓐ colorful
   - Ⓑ made from plants
   - Ⓒ easy to wash
   - Ⓓ only one color

2. Many plants we eat _____.
   - Ⓐ need to be soaked in water
   - Ⓑ are not found in nature
   - Ⓒ all make red dye
   - Ⓓ can be used as dyes

3. Which is likely true about colors in nature?
   - Ⓐ They are hard to find.
   - Ⓑ There is a wide variety.
   - Ⓒ They are hard to see.
   - Ⓓ They are all dark.

4. Based on the passage, what can you tell about people from long ago?
   - Ⓐ They liked to cook.
   - Ⓑ They did not eat carrots.
   - Ⓒ They used things from nature.
   - Ⓓ They liked green clothes best.

STRATEGY PRACTICE Write the name of three plants and the colors they make.

_____

_____

Name: _____

READ THE PASSAGE Find out what you would do if you were a "rock hound."

Rock Hound

People like to collect different things. Some collect stamps. Some collect dolls. Sandy's brother collects pennies. He has some that are over 50 years old.

Sandy is a "rock hound." She likes to look for rocks. She learns everything she can about the rocks she finds. She keeps all her rocks in a special place.

One of Sandy's rocks is called shale. It is flat and gray. It is made from clay that was pressed together over many, many years. Sandy has another rock that is shiny black with sharp edges like glass. It was formed from the lava of a volcano.

Sandy and her father take hikes together. They pick up interesting rocks. At home, Sandy looks in her rock book to find a picture of each new rock. Then she writes its name on a label and adds the new treasure to the others on her shelf.

SKILL PRACTICE Read the question. Fill in the bubble next to the correct answer.

1. Sandy and her brother both like to _____.
   Ⓐ take hikes
   Ⓑ collect things
   Ⓒ look for pennies
   Ⓓ learn about rocks

2. How is Sandy's collection different from her brother's?
   Ⓐ Her collection is from nature, but his is not.
   Ⓑ She collects glass, but he does not.
   Ⓒ She collects pictures of rocks, but he does not.
   Ⓓ She collects old things, but he does not.

3. Sandy could probably tell you _____.
   Ⓐ who sells old dolls
   Ⓑ how coins are made
   Ⓒ how rocks are formed
   Ⓓ where to find treasure

4. Which of these is most likely true about Sandy?
   Ⓐ She collects things made of clay.
   Ⓑ She wants a different collection.
   Ⓒ She wants to be like her brother.
   Ⓓ She likes to hike with her father.

STRATEGY PRACTICE Write a question that can be answered by the passage. Have a partner answer your question.

Character and Setting

Students study a passage to better understand who or what is at the center of the action and when and where the action takes place.

Fantasy and Reality

Students identify which things in the passage could or could not happen in real life.

DAY 1

Review the *Character and Setting* skill with students. Say: **The characters are who a story or passage is mostly about. The setting is where and when a story or passage takes place.** Tell students they are going to read a story about two girls who have a problem. Read the instructions at the top of the page aloud. Then remind students of the *Make Connections* strategy, which was taught during Week 1. Say: **It is easier to understand what the characters do and how they feel when you recall similar things that you may have done or seen.** Direct students to read the passage and to complete the skill practice activity. Review the answers together. For the strategy practice activity, pair students or complete it as a group. Note: The joke referred to in the story is *Did you hear about the cross-eyed teacher? He couldn't control his pupils.*

DAY 2

Remind students of the *Character and Setting* skill. Tell students they are going to read about what two friends find to do on a rainy day. Read the instructions at the top of the page aloud. Remind students of the *Visualization* strategy, which was taught during Week 2. Say: **Making a mental picture of the characters and setting will help you understand and remember what you read.** Direct students to read the passage and to complete the skill practice activities. Review the answers together. For the strategy practice activity, pair students or complete it as a group.

DAY 3

Review the *Fantasy and Reality* skill with students. Say: **When something happens in a story that could happen or exist in real life, it is reality. Things that could not happen or exist in real life are fantasy.** Read the instructions at the top of the page aloud, and point out that there must be something in the story that is fantasy. Remind students of the *Make Connections* strategy, and instruct them to notice things in the story that are similar to other fantasy stories they know. Have students read the passage. Discuss what similarities to other fantasy stories students noticed. Then direct students to complete the skill practice activity, and review the answers together. For the strategy practice activity, pair students or complete it as a group.

DAY 4

Remind students of the *Fantasy and Reality* skill. Read the instructions at the top of the page aloud. Then read the title of the passage. Ask students to speculate on what they will read about and what might be fantasy. Remind students to use *Visualization* to help them form clear ideas about what is happening. Direct students to read the passage and to complete the skill and strategy practice activities. Review the answers together. For the strategy practice activity, call on a volunteer to read the sentence that creates the best mental picture. Discuss which phrases helped them visualize how Pat felt (e.g., "*dropped the bat with a thump;*" "*dragged her feet*").

DAY 5

Tell students they will practice both the *Character and Setting* and *Fantasy and Reality* skills. Review the skills if necessary. Then read the instructions at the top of the page aloud. Remind students to make connections between themselves and the characters and events to better understand the story. Have students read the passage. When students have finished, direct them to complete the skill practice activity. Review the answers together. For the strategy practice activity, pair students or complete it as a group.

READ THE PASSAGE Think about what the girls should do.

The Giggles

Ava and Jill went to the library during recess. They looked at a favorite joke book together. When Jill read the joke about the cross-eyed teacher, Ava started giggling. That started Jill giggling. The girls couldn't stop. The librarian told them to leave.

When the bell rang, the girls returned to the classroom. They sat down at their desks. Ava covered her mouth and took a deep breath. Miss Ling started the math lesson. When she started writing on the board, the piece of chalk broke. This made the girls giggle some more. "That is enough, girls," Miss Ling said. Ava felt sorry, but she could not stop laughing.

Miss Ling moved Ava to the back of the room. Ava finally stopped laughing. She was careful not to look at Jill. She knew that if she did, she would start giggling all over again.

SKILL PRACTICE Read the question. Fill in the bubble next to the correct answer.

1. The passage begins _____.
   - Ⓐ at Ava's house
   - Ⓑ in the school library
   - Ⓒ in the girls' classroom
   - Ⓓ on the playground at recess

2. Most of the passage takes place _____.
   - Ⓐ in the school library
   - Ⓑ on a playground at school
   - Ⓒ in a classroom
   - Ⓓ at Miss Ling's house

3. Where are the girls when they start laughing?
   - Ⓐ at their desks
   - Ⓑ in the lunch area
   - Ⓒ near their classroom
   - Ⓓ in the library

4. How does Ava feel when she is moved to the back of the room?
   - Ⓐ sorry
   - Ⓑ angry
   - Ⓒ bored
   - Ⓓ silly

STRATEGY PRACTICE Tell a partner about a time when you had the giggles like Ava.

READ THE PASSAGE   Pay attention to the different places in the passage.

Rainy Day

Zack and his friend Noah were tired of playing board games and watching TV. Noah looked out the window at the gray day. "It's still raining," he said.

"Let's go outside," said Zack. "Never mind the rain!" The boys put on their yellow raincoats and boots. Then they went out to the backyard to play.

First, they threw the football. Zack slid on the grass and laughed. Next, they went on the swings. When they swung up high, the rain sprinkled their faces. Then, the boys went down the slide. They landed in a puddle at the bottom.

Both boys climbed the ladder to the red, wooden treehouse and watched the rain fall all around. It made a quiet, pattering sound on the green leaves above their heads.

"The rain is fun," said Zack.

"It's time for lunch," called Zack's mother from the house. "Come in for hot soup and sandwiches."

SKILL PRACTICE   Read the question. Fill in the bubble next to the correct answer.

1. Most of the passage happens _____.

   Ⓐ at a park

   Ⓑ at a school

   Ⓒ in a backyard

   Ⓓ at a playground

2. Which words describe the boys?

   Ⓐ tired, then hungry

   Ⓑ bored, then having fun

   Ⓒ hungry, then tired

   Ⓓ wet, then dry

3. Where are the boys when they land in a puddle?

   Ⓐ near the swings

   Ⓑ under the treehouse

   Ⓒ outside the back door

   Ⓓ at the bottom of the slide

4. Which word best describes Zack?

   Ⓐ playful

   Ⓑ sleepy

   Ⓒ scared

   Ⓓ unfriendly

STRATEGY PRACTICE   Tell a partner about two things you pictured in the passage.

READ THE PASSAGE Think about what could and could not be real.

The Pearl Divers

Once upon a time, two children lived with their mother in a little hut by the sea. Their mother washed clothes for the people on the island. She was always very tired. The children wished their mother didn't have to work so hard.

Every day, the children dove for oysters in the sea. They opened the shells to look for pearls growing inside. They would sell the pearls for a lot of money.

One day, while the children were diving for oysters, they saw a mermaid sitting on a rock. When she asked the children what they were doing, they told her their story.

"I can help you," the mermaid said. "Follow me!" She leaped into the water and swam away, her shiny tail waving behind her.

The children put on their fins and masks. They followed the mermaid to a small, hidden beach. In the sand was a box filled with treasure.

"Oh, thank you!" cried the children. "Now our mother won't have to work."

SKILL PRACTICE Read the question. Fill in the bubble next to the correct answer.

1. The passage is about two children who _____.
   - Ⓐ build a nice house
   - Ⓑ want to help their mother
   - Ⓒ find a perfect pearl
   - Ⓓ bury a treasure box

2. Which one <u>cannot</u> really happen?
   - Ⓐ wearing a mask
   - Ⓑ looking for pearls
   - Ⓒ living on an island
   - Ⓓ talking to a mermaid

3. Which one is hardest to believe?
   - Ⓐ Children find treasure.
   - Ⓑ Children make friends.
   - Ⓒ Children swim in the water.
   - Ⓓ Children help their mother.

4. Which one is make-believe?
   - Ⓐ swim fins
   - Ⓑ an island hut
   - Ⓒ a mermaid
   - Ⓓ an oyster shell

STRATEGY PRACTICE Tell a partner what you would do if you found buried treasure.

READ THE PASSAGE Notice where the passage becomes make-believe.

Pat at Bat

"Strike!" called the umpire. Pat squeezed the neck of the smooth, wooden bat as she waited for the next pitch. *Swoosh!* Pat swung and missed. The ball bounced behind her, sending up a cloud of dust. The catcher scooped it up and threw it back to the pitcher.

"Strike three—You're OUT!" Pat's heart sank. She dropped the bat to the ground with a thump and dragged her feet as she walked to the bench.

That night, while eating apple pie, Pat told Grandpa about her problem. "No matter how hard I try," she said, "I cannot hit the ball. Can you help me?" Grandpa did not say a word. He got up and left the room. When he returned, he was holding an old, dirty baseball.

"This baseball is magic," Grandpa said to Pat. "You will be able to hit it."

He was right! When Grandpa pitched the old ball to Pat, it flew to her bat like a magnet. She hit it every time. Pat's batting got better and better. Soon, she could hit any ball.

SKILL PRACTICE Read the question. Fill in the bubble next to the correct answer.

1. The passage is mostly about a _____.

    Ⓐ big baseball game

    Ⓑ girl running fast

    Ⓒ girl solving her problem

    Ⓓ famous baseball player

2. Which one is make-believe?

    Ⓐ a ball that flies to a bat

    Ⓑ a girl who plays baseball

    Ⓒ a man who helps a girl bat

    Ⓓ a grandpa who has an old baseball

3. Which one is hardest to believe?

    Ⓐ asking someone for help

    Ⓑ hitting the ball every time

    Ⓒ being sad about a problem

    Ⓓ getting better at a skill

4. Which one from the passage is magic?

    Ⓐ Pat's bat

    Ⓑ the apple pie

    Ⓒ Pat's grandpa

    Ⓓ Grandpa's old baseball

STRATEGY PRACTICE Underline the sentence that helps you picture how Pat felt when she struck out.

READ THE PASSAGE   What parts of the passage could and could not happen?

The Lincoln Statue

It was springtime. The cherry trees were pink with fluffy blossoms. Meg and her family were on a trip to Washington, D.C. They saw the White House, where the president lives. They walked along the great mall with its long, green lawn.

Meg and her family climbed the wide stairs of the Lincoln Memorial. The building had tall white columns in front. Inside was a giant statue of Abraham Lincoln sitting in a chair. Meg felt tiny beside the statue. As she stared up at it, she thought she saw the statue wink.

"How could he be so important?" asked Meg's sister. "He isn't alive anymore."

"Lincoln worked to save this country," Meg's father said. "His ideas are very important." As her family turned to leave, Meg stayed for one more moment. She looked up at the statue. Its lips began to move!

"Remember, Meg," said Lincoln, "you can do something for your country, too."

SKILL PRACTICE   Read the question. Fill in the bubble next to the correct answer.

1. **Where does the passage take place?**
   - Ⓐ in Washington, D.C.
   - Ⓑ at a park
   - Ⓒ at a shopping mall
   - Ⓓ at the president's home

2. **Which description matches Meg's father?**
   - Ⓐ afraid of the statue
   - Ⓑ proud of his country
   - Ⓒ confused by his daughter
   - Ⓓ surprised by the White House

3. **Which one is magic?**
   - Ⓐ A girl looks up at a statue.
   - Ⓑ A president had great ideas.
   - Ⓒ A big statue winks at a little girl.
   - Ⓓ A family sees the White House.

4. **Which one cannot be real?**
   - Ⓐ trees with pink blossoms
   - Ⓑ wide stairs outside a building
   - Ⓒ a family on a trip
   - Ⓓ a statue that talks

STRATEGY PRACTICE   Tell a partner something you know about your country's history.

Author's Purpose
Students think about why an author wrote a particular passage.

Prediction
Students use clues from the text and their own background knowledge to anticipate what is likely to happen next or what information will come next.

DAY 1

Review the *Author's Purpose* skill with students. Say: **When we know why the author wrote what we are reading, it is easier to understand the main ideas of the passage or story.** Then remind students of the common reasons why authors write: to give information, to entertain, to tell how to do something, or to persuade. Remind students of the *Ask Questions* strategy, which was taught during Week 5. Say: **Asking questions about information as you read will help you get more involved in the story and notice information you don't understand.** Read the instructions at the top of the page aloud. Then have students read the passage. Discuss the author's purpose (to give information about a boy who does something to help others). Direct students to complete the skill practice activity. Review the answers together. Then direct students to complete the strategy practice activity. Invite volunteers to share their responses.

DAY 2

Remind students of the *Author's Purpose* skill, and review the most common purposes: to give information, to tell a story that entertains, to tell how to do something, and to persuade. Read the instructions at the top of the page aloud. Remind students of the *Make Connections* strategy, which was taught during Week 1. Say: **The title tells us that this story is about a little house. As you read, think about how the place in the story is like one you may have seen. This will help you understand what the author is saying.** Then direct students to read the passage and to complete the skill practice activity. For the strategy practice activity, pair students or complete it as a group.

DAY 3

Review the *Prediction* skill with students. Say: **When we predict, we use information from the passage and our own experiences to make a good guess about what is likely to happen next.** Hold up a glass or cup full of water. Ask: **What will happen if I pour the water onto a stack of papers?** (The papers will get wet or will be ruined.) **You know that will happen because you've seen it happen before. You used your experiences to make a prediction of what will happen next.** Tell students they will read about what happens to a girl named Lupe, who is forgetful. Remind students of the *Ask Questions* strategy. Say: **As you read, ask yourself questions about Lupe and what she does so that you understand what is happening.** Then read the instructions at the top of the page aloud. Direct students to read the passage and to complete the activities. Review the answers together, and invite volunteers to share their responses to the strategy practice activity.

DAY 4

Remind students of both the *Prediction* skill and the *Make Connections* strategy. Say: **By making connections, you use past experiences to help you understand what you read. These connections also help you make predictions.** Read the instructions at the top of the page aloud. Direct students to read the passage and to complete the skill practice activity. Review the answers together. For the strategy practice activity, pair students or complete it as a group.

DAY 5

Tell students they will practice both the *Author's Purpose* and *Prediction* skills. If necessary, review the definitions of each skill. Then remind students of the *Ask Questions* strategy. Read the instructions at the top of the page aloud. Then say: **You will also want to ask yourself questions about what may happen next.** Have students read the passage. When students have finished, direct them to complete the skill practice activity. For the strategy practice activity, pair students or complete it as a group.

READ THE PASSAGE   Ask yourself why the author wrote the passage.

Kid Hero

What is a hero? A hero is a person who is brave and good. A hero is looked up to by others. Joey Athey is a hero. If you met him, you would notice his kindness. You would see how hard he works. You would see that he likes to make other children happy.

When Joey was in kindergarten, his school started a project. Each student was asked to do something for others without wanting anything in return. This took some clever thinking!

Joey wanted to give toys to children whose families could not buy them toys. He baked some cookies. Then he sold them. With the money he earned, Joey bought some toys. Then he gave the toys to poor children.

Joey has been selling cookies for almost six years! Because of him, many children are having fun with new toys. "I hope I will always do this," says Joey.

SKILL PRACTICE   Read the question. Fill in the bubble next to the correct answer.

1. Why does the author call Joey a hero?
    Ⓐ Joey's idea is clever.
    Ⓑ Joey knows how to bake cookies.
    Ⓒ Joey works to help others.
    Ⓓ Joey earns money.

2. The author thinks that Joey is _____.
    Ⓐ kind
    Ⓑ funny
    Ⓒ rich
    Ⓓ brave

3. According to the author, a hero is someone who _____.
    Ⓐ bakes cookies
    Ⓑ is brave and good
    Ⓒ is in kindergarten
    Ⓓ buys toys

4. What is the most likely reason the author wrote the passage?
    Ⓐ to describe nice toys
    Ⓑ to explain how to bake cookies
    Ⓒ to tell a story about happy children
    Ⓓ to tell about a boy who helps others

STRATEGY PRACTICE   What is a question you would ask Joey Athey?

_____

READ THE PASSAGE Ask yourself why the author wrote the passage.

The Little House

A little house stands on a very nice street. The people who live in the little house keep the yellow paint bright and fresh. They keep the windows clean. Every Saturday, the man mows and waters the grass. His wife tends the flowers and bushes that grow along the front of the house. The children who live in the little house help, too. They sweep the steps and the walkway.

The little house has leafy green trees all around it. The children and their friends climb the trees. They play on a swing that hangs from a large branch. Birds build nests in the trees. Squirrels leap from branch to branch near the tops of the trees.

Lacy curtains hang in the windows of the little house. Each holiday season, the children cut out decorations and hang them in the windows. People smile when they walk by the little house. They can tell that the owners love their home.

SKILL PRACTICE Read the question. Fill in the bubble next to the correct answer.

1. Why did the author write the passage?
   Ⓐ to explain how to paint a house
   Ⓑ to describe a house to others
   Ⓒ to tell a sad story about a house
   Ⓓ to make people want to buy a house

2. Which of these does the author not tell about?
   Ⓐ what the house looks like
   Ⓑ what the trees look like
   Ⓒ what the family does on Saturdays
   Ⓓ what the family cooks for dinner

3. Which of these do you think the author would say?
   Ⓐ "You can tell when people care about their home."
   Ⓑ "Yellow is a good color for a house."
   Ⓒ "Lacy curtains are the best kind."
   Ⓓ "Kids should not help clean house."

4. Why does the author describe the trees?
   Ⓐ to compare trees to houses
   Ⓑ to explain how to grow trees
   Ⓒ to help you picture the trees
   Ⓓ to tell a story about birds

STRATEGY PRACTICE Tell a partner what you would like best about the little house if you lived in it.

READ THE PASSAGE   What do you think Lupe will do next?

Trip Slip

"Don't forget your trip slip," Lupe's mother said.

"I won't, Mom!" called Lupe from the kitchen.

"That's what you said yesterday and on Monday, too," Mom called back.

"I'll remember it," Lupe said. She ate her cereal, picked up her backpack, and left for school. Later, her mother saw something on the kitchen table.

"Oh, dear," thought Lupe's mother.

At school, Lupe's teacher asked the class if there was anyone who had not turned in their trip slips. Lupe and two other students raised their hands.

"Remember," said Lupe's teacher, "if you do not bring in a slip signed by a parent, you cannot go on the class trip to the zoo tomorrow."

Not go on the trip? Lupe made up her mind. She would not forget her trip slip again. That night, she put it in the zippered pocket of the jacket she always wore.

SKILL PRACTICE   Read the question. Fill in the bubble next to the correct answer.

1. Why do you think Lupe's mother says, "Oh, dear"?

   Ⓐ Lupe leaves the cereal open.

   Ⓑ Lupe forgets her trip slip again.

   Ⓒ Lupe forgets her backpack.

   Ⓓ Lupe's mother forgot to eat breakfast.

2. What do you think Lupe will do tomorrow?

   Ⓐ go to the zoo alone

   Ⓑ forget her backpack

   Ⓒ ask her mother for help

   Ⓓ take her trip slip to school

3. What do you think Lupe's teacher will do tomorrow?

   Ⓐ ask the three students for their slips

   Ⓑ send the class to the zoo by themselves

   Ⓒ say the trip is called off

   Ⓓ drive the bus to the zoo

4. What do you think will happen if Lupe forgets her trip slip again?

   Ⓐ She will go to the zoo.

   Ⓑ Lupe's teacher will sign the slip.

   Ⓒ She will not go to the zoo.

   Ⓓ The class will stay at school.

STRATEGY PRACTICE   What is one question you asked as you read about Lupe?

_____

READ THE PASSAGE Think about what the kids will do next.

Where Is Kitty?

"Kitty, where are you?" Jake and Iris could not find their cat.

The family had moved across town a month before. Kitty seemed confused at first, but soon she seemed to feel at home. Now she had disappeared.

"I'll check the neighborhood," said Iris. She went to the garage where her bike was. Jake remembered seeing lots of posters for missing pets at the park. He got markers and paper.

The phone rang. Mom answered it. When she hung up, Mom talked to Dad.

"Our neighbor from the old house called," Mom said as she picked up her car keys.

"That silly cat must still be confused." Dad smiled and went to find the children.

SKILL PRACTICE Read the question. Fill in the bubble next to the correct answer.

1. **What will Mom probably do next?**
   Ⓐ get another cat
   Ⓑ go to the old house
   Ⓒ look for Kitty with Iris
   Ⓓ have lunch with Dad

2. **What will Dad probably do next?**
   Ⓐ tell the children Kitty was found
   Ⓑ help Jake with his homework
   Ⓒ tell Mom not to leave
   Ⓓ help Iris fix her bike

3. **Why do you think Jake gets markers and paper?**
   Ⓐ to do his homework
   Ⓑ to draw a picture for Iris
   Ⓒ to make a card for the neighbor from the old house
   Ⓓ to make a poster that tells Kitty is missing

4. **What do you think might happen if Kitty is missing again?**
   Ⓐ The family will get a new cat.
   Ⓑ Jake and Iris will ask for a dog.
   Ⓒ The family will look near its old house.
   Ⓓ The neighbor will keep Kitty.

STRATEGY PRACTICE Tell a partner about a time you lost something important and what you did.

Think about what will happen next.

New Shoes

Mario needed a new pair of shoes. Holes were forming near the big toes of the old ones.

Mario's mother took him to the store. A salesperson measured Mario's feet. "Your feet are Size 2," the salesperson said to Mario.

"I only wore Size 1 last year!" said Mario. The man smiled. Mario looked at the shoes on the shelf. He chose two different pairs to try on. One pair was black. The other was blue. The salesperson brought two boxes. Each box held a Size 2 pair of the shoes that Mario had chosen.

Mario tried on the two pairs of shoes. The black ones pinched his toes when he walked, but the blue ones felt just right. Mario walked back and forth in the store. He jumped, and then he stood on his toes.

"I want to wear these shoes to school tomorrow!" exclaimed Mario.

SKILL PRACTICE Read the question. Fill in the bubble next to the correct answer.

1. Why did the author write the passage?
   - Ⓐ to tell a story
   - Ⓑ to describe a shoe store
   - Ⓒ to teach how to buy shoes
   - Ⓓ to make people want new shoes

2. What do you think happens next?
   - Ⓐ Mario's feet start to hurt.
   - Ⓑ Mario gives the shoes back.
   - Ⓒ Mario's mom buys the shoes.
   - Ⓓ Mario goes to a different store.

3. Why does the author tell what shoe size Mario wore last year?
   - Ⓐ to show that Mario is a year older
   - Ⓑ to show that Mario is confused
   - Ⓒ to show that Mario knows his numbers
   - Ⓓ to show that Mario's feet have grown

4. Where will the black shoes probably go now?
   - Ⓐ into a trash can
   - Ⓑ back in the box
   - Ⓒ to another store
   - Ⓓ home with Mario

STRATEGY PRACTICE Tell a partner a question you have about Mario's new shoes.

Nonfiction Text Features

Students look at text features, such as headings and captions, to better understand what they read.

Visual Information

Students discover how pictures, charts, graphs, and other visual elements can explain more about a topic.

DAY 1

Remind students that nonfiction text features are related to the main body of text in a passage but different from it. Tell students they will be reading a flier, which is a printed piece of paper that gives information or advertises something. Show samples of fliers, and point out the nonfiction text features (headings, bold-print words, etc.). Then remind students of the *Determine Important Information* strategy, which was taught during Week 4. Explain that looking for nonfiction text features can help to identify which information is most important. Then read the instructions at the top of the page aloud. Read the flier aloud as a class, calling on individuals to read various sections, and pointing out the headlines as nonfiction text features. Direct students to complete the skill practice activity, and then review the answers together. Complete the strategy practice activity as a group, asking students to give reasons for their choices.

DAY 2

Remind students of the *Nonfiction Text Features* skill. Then remind them of the *Organization* strategy, which was taught during Week 3. Say: **Nonfiction text features can be organized in a way to make information easier to find.** Read the instructions at the top of the page aloud. Ask students to look at the schedule and determine what kind of information it is (information for students of an art school). Read the schedule aloud together. Call students' attention to the headings, and discuss what information they give. Direct students to complete the skill practice activity, and review the answers together. Complete the strategy practice activity as a group, introducing students to the phrase *chronological order* to describe the way the information is organized.

DAY 3

Remind students that visual information is information that can be given as pictures, graphs, charts, and maps, and that sometimes visual information is easier and quicker to understand than text. Tell students they are going to study a menu for a snack bar at a fair. Remind students of the *Determine Important Information* strategy. Read the instructions at the top of the page aloud. Ask for volunteers to read parts of the menu. As each part is read, decide as a group if that information is important to know if you wanted to order a snack. Direct students to complete the skill practice activity independently. Review the answers together. Then direct students to complete the strategy practice activity and share their responses.

DAY 4

Review that *visual information* is the term for non-word features such as pictures, maps, and graphs. Ask students if they have ever used a map to help them find their way around a park or a mall. Allow time for students to share experiences. Remind students of the *Organization* strategy. Say: **Maps are organized to show places located just as they are in the world. If a place on a map is to the right of another place, you know it is that way in reality.** Guide students through the museum map, having volunteers read the text. Discuss the location of each room relative to the others. Direct students to complete the activities, and then review the answers together.

DAY 5

Tell students they will practice both the *Nonfiction Text Features* and *Visual Information* skills. Remind students of the *Determine Important Information* strategy. Say: **Studying nonfiction text features and visual information will help you determine which information is important.** Ask students to identify the type of passage they will be reading (recipe). Guide students through the passage. Then direct students to complete the activities independently. Review the answers together.

READ THE FLIER   Look for information that seems the most important.

The Place for Fall Fun!

You can do lots of fun activities
at Apple Farm Day Camp:

- Feed the chickens.
- See how horseshoes are made.
- Pick apples, make cider, and bake pies.
- Sing songs around a campfire.
- Make arts and crafts.

When
Every Saturday in October
10:00 a.m. to 4:00 p.m.

Where
Apple Farm, 1111 Foothill Road

How to Join
Bring a parent to the Apple Farm
office and sign up.

What to Wear
Jeans and a sweater

SKILL PRACTICE   Read the question. Fill in the bubble next to the correct answer.

1. What is the reason for the headline
   at the top of the flier?

   Ⓐ to fill the space

   Ⓑ to tell you the time of year

   Ⓒ to get you interested

   Ⓓ to tell you what to do

2. The words in bold print help you
   by _____.

   Ⓐ being at the beginning of the line

   Ⓑ pointing out important information

   Ⓒ starting with a capital letter

   Ⓓ not being sentences

3. What is one thing campers can do
   at Apple Farm Day Camp?

   Ⓐ make crafts

   Ⓑ plant seeds

   Ⓒ collect eggs

   Ⓓ build fences

4. Which one must you do to join?

   Ⓐ have a sweater

   Ⓑ know how to bake a pie

   Ⓒ like arts and crafts

   Ⓓ have a parent come with you

STRATEGY PRACTICE   Underline information you would need to know if you
wanted to go to Apple Farm Day Camp.

READ THE SCHEDULE Look for features that help you understand the information.

Nature Art School

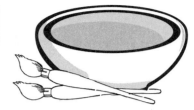

Welcome to Nature Art School!
We will make something new each week.

Week 1: Clay
We will make beautiful coil bowls. Then we'll bake them in a pottery oven.

Week 2: String
We will decorate greeting cards with string art.

Week 3: Rocks
We will paint flat rocks and turn them into beautiful paperweights.

Week 4: Sand
We will make sand candles and color them to make them blue.

SKILL PRACTICE Read the question. Fill in the bubble next to the correct answer.

1. The art classes last for _____.

   Ⓐ one year

   Ⓑ four days

   Ⓒ four weeks

   Ⓓ two months

2. The words in bold print tell _____.

   Ⓐ where the classes are each week

   Ⓑ who will teach classes each week

   Ⓒ when classes are held each week

   Ⓓ what materials will be used each week

3. In Week 3, the class will _____.

   Ⓐ paint rocks

   Ⓑ paint bowls

   Ⓒ make cards

   Ⓓ make candles

4. When will the class use string?

   Ⓐ Week 1

   Ⓑ Week 2

   Ⓒ Week 3

   Ⓓ Week 4

STRATEGY PRACTICE In what order was the information given?

_____

READ THE MENU How does the visual information help you understand the menu?

SKILL PRACTICE Read the question. Fill in the bubble next to the correct answer.

1. **How many different prices are there at the Snack Shack?**

   Ⓐ three

   Ⓑ eight

   Ⓒ two

   Ⓓ seven

2. **How do the pictures help you?**

   Ⓐ They make the menu pretty.

   Ⓑ You do not have to read the words.

   Ⓒ You can tell which food tastes best.

   Ⓓ You can tell what rides are at the fair.

3. **What information is given about the food and drinks on the menu?**

   Ⓐ what they taste like

   Ⓑ where to find them

   Ⓒ who is selling them

   Ⓓ what they look like

4. **Which of these foods is named after a ride?**

   Ⓐ corn dog

   Ⓑ cotton candy

   Ⓒ fries

   Ⓓ sandwich

STRATEGY PRACTICE Which information is most important if you have only a certain amount of money to spend?

_____

READ THE MAP   Think about how the pictures help you read the map.

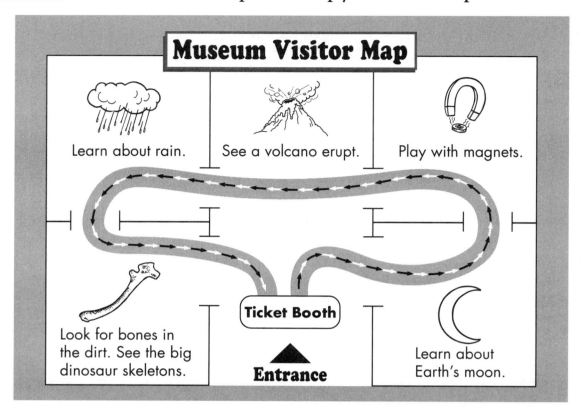

SKILL PRACTICE   Read the question. Fill in the bubble next to the correct answer.

1. Information about the exhibits is given by the captions and _____.

　Ⓐ the person in the ticket booth

　Ⓑ a sign at the entrance

　Ⓒ the pictures on the map

　Ⓓ the title on the map

2. Where is the ticket booth?

　Ⓐ outside the entrance

　Ⓑ just inside the entrance

　Ⓒ in the back of the museum

　Ⓓ inside and to the left of the entrance

3. What do visitors learn about first?

　Ⓐ the moon

　Ⓑ dinosaurs

　Ⓒ volcanoes

　Ⓓ the weather

4. After visitors learn about rain, they _____.

　Ⓐ play with magnets

　Ⓑ leave the museum

　Ⓒ watch a volcano form

　Ⓓ dig for dinosaur bones

STRATEGY PRACTICE   How do visitors know the order in which to see the museum exhibits?

_____

READ THE RECIPE Notice the features that help you make sense of the information.

Banana Bread

Tools You Need	Ingredients	What to Do
• large mixing bowl • wooden spoon • measuring cup • 8" x 4" loaf pan 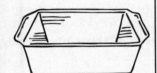	3 ripe bananas $\frac{1}{3}$ cup of melted butter 1 cup of sugar 1 egg 1 teaspoon of vanilla 1 teaspoon of baking soda 1 pinch of salt $1\frac{1}{2}$ cups of flour	1. Ask a parent to heat the oven to 350°. 2. Squish up the banana and butter. 3. Add the sugar, egg, and vanilla. 4. Add the baking soda, salt, and flour. 5. Mix the ingredients with the spoon. 6. Pour the batter into the loaf pan. 7. Bake for one hour. 8. Cool, slice, and enjoy!

SKILL PRACTICE Read the question. Fill in the bubble next to the correct answer.

1. **What kind of information is shown?**

   Ⓐ a recipe

   Ⓑ a picnic list

   Ⓒ a party food plan

   Ⓓ a restaurant menu

2. **What does the picture tell you?**

   Ⓐ all the tools you need

   Ⓑ what the recipe will make

   Ⓒ what size the loaf pan should be

   Ⓓ what a loaf pan looks like

3. **Which step tells to stir the batter?**

   Ⓐ step 8

   Ⓑ step 3

   Ⓒ step 5

   Ⓓ step 4

4. **What do the numbers in bold print tell you?**

   Ⓐ how many tools you need

   Ⓑ the order in which to make the bread

   Ⓒ which part of the recipe matters most

   Ⓓ how long it will take to make the recipe

STRATEGY PRACTICE Circle the heading you will look under to find the food items you need.

Main Idea and Details

Students look for the central idea or message of a passage or story. They also find details that best support the main idea.

Sequence

Students look for the order of events or steps in a process.

DAY 1

Review the *Main Idea and Details* skill with students. Say: **Remember that the *main idea* is what the passage is mostly about. Ideas that tell us more about the main idea are called *details*.** Read the instructions at the top of the page aloud. Then remind students of the *Monitor Comprehension* strategy, taught during Week 6. Say: **As good readers, we stop while reading and ask, *What is the most important idea of the part I just read?*** Have students read the passage. When they have finished, direct them to complete the skill practice activity, and review the answers together. For the strategy practice activity, pair students or complete it as a group.

DAY 2

Remind students of the *Main Idea and Details* skill and the *Determine Important Information* strategy (Week 4). Then read the instructions at the top of the page aloud. Say: **It's important to notice which details tell important things and which details are not important, even though they may be interesting.** Call on volunteers to read the passage aloud. Stop after each paragraph to clarify information that may be new to students. Determine as a group what each paragraph was about (Hush puppies are crispy balls of cornmeal, flour, and egg. One legend says hush puppies got their name because soldiers used them to keep their dogs quiet. The name may come from fishermen who fed them to their dogs.). Direct students to complete the skill practice activity independently. Review the answers together. For the strategy practice activity, pair students or complete it as a group.

DAY 3

Review the *Sequence* skill with students. Say: **We are going to read about how to make candles. Remember that when you read about how to do something, it's important to pay attention to the order of the steps. Good readers stop while reading to monitor comprehension. They ask themselves if they remember the sequence of events.** Read the passage aloud together, and then complete the skill practice activity as a group. Pair students to complete the strategy practice activity. Monitor the pairs to point out any missed steps.

DAY 4

Remind students of the *Sequence* skill. Say: **When we read about the life of a real person, the events are usually told in the order they happened. Often, dates are given in order. We call this *chronological order*. Looking for dates can help you determine important information. You are going to read about a famous American named Thomas Edison.** Read the instructions at the top of the page aloud. Read the passage aloud together, clarifying facts and concepts for students. Direct students to complete the skill practice activity independently. Review the answers together. Then complete the strategy practice activity as a group.

DAY 5

Tell students they will practice both the *Main Idea and Details* and *Sequence* skills as they read about a strange ocean creature. Read the instructions at the top of the page aloud. Remind students to use the *Monitor Comprehension* strategy to help them notice the information. Say: **As you read, ask yourself, *Do I remember the important ideas? Can I repeat what I'm reading in the correct order?*** Direct students to read the passage and to complete the skill and strategy practice activities. Review the answers together.

Find out about a different kind of duck.

When Is a Truck a Duck?

Imagine that you are riding in a car. It comes to the edge of a river. It drives down a ramp. *Whoosh!* The car goes into the water and begins to glide along the shore. You must be riding in a "duck."

You may think these special vehicles are known as ducks because they can go in and out of the water like the bird. Not so. The first ducks were built during the Second World War. They carried soldiers and supplies from ships to land in places where there were no docks. They were called by the letters DUKW. Because of this spelling, people started calling them "ducks."

Since then, new kinds of ducks have been built. They are much more comfortable to ride in. Many cities on rivers use ducks to give rides to visitors. You can see the city sights from the streets and from the water, too.

SKILL PRACTICE   Read the question. Fill in the bubble next to the correct answer.

1. What is the passage mostly about?
   - Ⓐ a special kind of truck
   - Ⓑ cities on rivers
   - Ⓒ ships that carry supplies
   - Ⓓ ducks that swim on rivers

2. The trucks in the passage got their name because _____.
   - Ⓐ the engine made a quacking sound
   - Ⓑ they looked like a water bird
   - Ⓒ they could go on land and on water
   - Ⓓ the letters they were called by sounded like "duck"

3. What were ducks first used for?
   - Ⓐ to drive through city streets
   - Ⓑ to take men and cargo to shore
   - Ⓒ to give rides to visitors
   - Ⓓ to build docks

4. What might you do if you rode in a duck?
   - Ⓐ feed birds at a zoo
   - Ⓑ go across the wide ocean
   - Ⓒ see the sights of a city
   - Ⓓ go in the desert

STRATEGY PRACTICE   Tell a partner how the "ducks" came to be.

READ THE PASSAGE Notice which sentences give the most important ideas.

A Food with a Funny Name

Hush puppies are small, crispy balls made of cornmeal, flour, and egg. They are a food that comes from the southern part of our country. Hush puppies are very tasty! People eat them with fried fish.

Hush puppies have a funny name. Where did it come from? One legend says that soldiers used hush puppies to keep their dogs quiet. Barking dogs could tell the enemy where to find the soldiers. As they tossed the crispy food to the dogs, the soldiers would say, "Hush, puppies!"

Here's another idea about where the name came from—Fishermen would make the fried balls when they cooked their catch over outdoor fires. They would toss a few treats to their whining dogs. The dogs would settle down and enjoy the hush puppies quietly.

SKILL PRACTICE Read the question. Fill in the bubble next to the correct answer.

1. What is the passage mostly about?
   Ⓐ barking dogs
   Ⓑ a kind of food
   Ⓒ a fun cookout
   Ⓓ soldiers who hide

2. What are hush puppies made of?
   Ⓐ fish
   Ⓑ chicken
   Ⓒ hot dogs
   Ⓓ cornmeal

3. Who tried to keep their dogs quiet?
   Ⓐ dog trainers
   Ⓑ corn growers
   Ⓒ soldiers
   Ⓓ restaurant owners

4. Hush puppies are often eaten with _____.
   Ⓐ fish
   Ⓑ corn
   Ⓒ chicken
   Ⓓ fried eggs

STRATEGY PRACTICE Underline the sentences that give the most important information about how hush puppies got their name. Read the sentences you underlined to a partner.

READ THE PASSAGE Find out what materials you need and what steps to follow.

How to Dip a Candle

Long before electric lights were invented, people used candles for light. They made the candles themselves. Making, or "dipping," a candle is easy and fun. You can do it, too.

First, gather your supplies. You will need a block of beeswax. You will need some crayons with the paper removed. You will also need two tall cans, a piece of cotton string as long as your arm, a wooden spoon, some newspaper, and a deep pot.

Next, spread the newspaper on a table. Fill one can with cold water. Put the wax in the other can. Add some crayon pieces for color. Ask a grown-up to place the can into a pot of boiling water. Stir the wax. Be sure the color is mixed well. Then dip the string into the wax. Dip it as deep as a ruler. Pull it out and dip it into the cold water. Then dip it into the wax again. Back and forth you go. The candle grows thicker and thicker. Cool your candle in cold water. Then trim the string. Make sure to leave a wick at the top to light.

SKILL PRACTICE Read the question. Fill in the bubble next to the correct answer.

1. **What is the first step?**
   - Ⓐ Leave a wick to light.
   - Ⓑ Dip the string into wax.
   - Ⓒ Fill a can with cold water.
   - Ⓓ Gather what you will need.

2. **Right after you put wax in a can, you _____.**
   - Ⓐ cool the candle
   - Ⓑ add pieces of crayon
   - Ⓒ spread out the newspaper
   - Ⓓ ask a grown-up for help

3. **After you dip the string in wax, you _____.**
   - Ⓐ find a spoon
   - Ⓑ cut it into pieces
   - Ⓒ dip it into a can of cold water
   - Ⓓ gather some newspaper

4. **Which step is last?**
   - Ⓐ Trim the wick.
   - Ⓑ Find a deep pot.
   - Ⓒ Measure your arm.
   - Ⓓ Dip the string in water.

STRATEGY PRACTICE Work with a partner. While one person reads the steps for dipping a candle, the other person acts them out.

READ THE PASSAGE Remember the events of Edison's life in order.

Thomas the Inventor

Thomas Alva Edison was a very curious child. He liked to know how things worked. Thomas liked to do experiments. He earned his own money for the supplies he needed. He sold candy and newspapers to people on a train.

When he was 27 years old, Thomas invented a new kind of telegraph. A telegraph is a machine that sends messages. The rich owner of a railroad paid Thomas $100,000 for the invention. With the money, Thomas built the first lab to be used just for inventing things. The building was in Menlo Park, New Jersey.

Edison invented the phonograph there in 1877. He recorded his own voice saying "Mary Had a Little Lamb." People were amazed at the phonograph. It seemed like magic. They called Edison "The Wizard of Menlo Park."

Edison was interested in the light bulb. The first light bulbs didn't last very long. Edison made a new kind of bulb that lasted longer than the others. He also found a way for the bulb to be used in houses and other buildings. Soon, New York City was bright with lights. Edison changed the world!

SKILL PRACTICE Read the question. Fill in the bubble next to the correct answer.

1. **What is the passage mostly about?**
   - Ⓐ machines that send messages
   - Ⓑ how electricity works
   - Ⓒ selling inventions for money
   - Ⓓ a famous inventor

2. **Edison invented a new telegraph _____.**
   - Ⓐ before he built his lab
   - Ⓑ after he invented the phonograph
   - Ⓒ after he made a new light bulb
   - Ⓓ before he sold candy on a train

3. **When did people start calling Edison "The Wizard of Menlo Park"?**
   - Ⓐ right after he made $100,000
   - Ⓑ after he invented the phonograph
   - Ⓒ after he made a better light bulb
   - Ⓓ when he was a young boy

4. **When did Edison record his own voice?**
   - Ⓐ before he made $100,000
   - Ⓑ after he invented the phonograph
   - Ⓒ after he made a better light bulb
   - Ⓓ before he sold newspapers

STRATEGY PRACTICE Underline the sentence in each paragraph that tells the main idea.

READ THE PASSAGE   Pay attention to what a green bomber is and how it drops "bombs."

Worms Drop Bombs

What's that, you say? There's a worm that drops bombs? It may sound strange, but it's true. The worms are called "green bombers." They are about four inches long and live very deep in the sea. A green bomber's body is mostly see-through. It is shaped like a long, thin brush. It has long bristles on each side of its body. These bristles work like paddles to move the worm through the water.

The green bomber swims along quietly until a hungry fish comes along. Then *kerplat!* The worm drops a "bomb." The bomb is actually a small part of its body. When it is dropped, the bomb glows bright green. If the fish bothers the worm, the worm drops more bombs. The glowing bombs confuse the fish. The worm swims safely away!

SKILL PRACTICE   Read the question. Fill in the bubble next to the correct answer.

1. **What is the passage about?**
   Ⓐ a surprising sea worm
   Ⓑ a plant that glows
   Ⓒ a fish that eats worms
   Ⓓ a see-through fish

2. **The green bomber moves by _____.**
   Ⓐ glowing green
   Ⓑ dropping parts of its body
   Ⓒ attaching itself to fish
   Ⓓ moving its bristles like paddles

3. **Which one happens first?**
   Ⓐ the bombs glow green
   Ⓑ the green bomber senses a fish
   Ⓒ the worm swims away
   Ⓓ the fish is confused

4. **What confuses the fish?**
   Ⓐ the little paddles
   Ⓑ the glowing parts
   Ⓒ the see-through worm
   Ⓓ the darkness of the sea

STRATEGY PRACTICE   In your own words, tell about the green bomber's bombs and why it drops them.

_____

_____

Cause and Effect
Students practice the skill by looking for what happens (the effect) and why it happens (the cause).

Fact and Opinion
Students determine whether parts of the passage can be proved (facts) or represent what someone thinks or feels (opinions).

DAY 1

Review the *Cause and Effect* skill with students. Say: **When something happens, it is the effect. The reason why it happens is the cause. Sometimes the cause and effect will be in the same sentence. Sometimes you will have to read further on in the passage to find the cause. It is important to read slowly and carefully to notice both the cause and its effect.** Read the instructions at the top of the page aloud. Then remind students of the *Visualization* strategy, which was taught during Week 2. Tell students that making a mental image of what happens is a good way to picture the causes and effects in a passage. Have students read the passage. When students have finished, direct them to complete the skill practice activity. Review the answers together. For the strategy practice activity, pair students or complete it as a group.

DAY 2

Remind students of the *Cause and Effect* skill and of the *Organization* strategy, which was taught during Week 3. Inform students that writers may organize their stories to have several causes and several effects, and that good readers pay attention to things that happen and why they happen. Read the instructions at the top of the page aloud. Then have students read the passage. When students have finished, direct them to complete the skill practice activity. Review the answers together. For the strategy practice activity, pair students or complete it as a group.

DAY 3

Review the *Fact and Opinion* skill with students. Say: **A fact can be proved. An opinion is what someone thinks or believes. It is a fact that there are four seasons. Can you name them?** *(winter, spring, summer, fall)* **If I tell you that summer is the best season, that is my opinion. You may think something different. Today we are going to find out what the writer of the passage thinks about the seasons.** Read the instructions at the top of the page aloud. Then remind students of the *Visualization* strategy and how it can help them determine what can be proved and what someone thinks. Direct students to read the passage and to complete the skill practice activity. Review the answers together. Complete the strategy practice activity as a group, asking students to give reasons for their choices.

DAY 4

Remind students of the *Fact and Opinion* skill. Read the instructions at the top of the page aloud. Then read the first paragraph aloud together. Point out the writer's four opinions about why cats are better pets than dogs. Remind students of the *Organization* strategy. Say: **One way a writer may organize a passage is to tell you his or her main opinions at the beginning and then tell you more about each opinion in the rest of the passage.** Direct students to read the passage and to complete the skill practice activity. Review the answers together. For the strategy practice activity, remind students that the writer gave four main opinions in the first paragraph and then told more about those opinions in the remaining paragraphs. Ask students to find and underline those opinions in paragraphs 2, 3, 4, and 5. Point out that all opinions are in the first sentence in each paragraph.

DAY 5

Tell students they will practice both the *Cause and Effect* and *Fact and Opinion* skills. Tell students they are going to read about two children who plant a garden. Say: **You will need to read carefully to find different cause-and-effect relationships, as well as examples of facts and opinions.** Remind students that using the *Visualization* strategy can help them notice the causes, effects, facts, and opinions in a passage. Then direct students to read the passage and to complete the skill and strategy practice activities. Review the answers together.

Daily Reading Comprehension • EMC 3452 • © Evan-Moor Corp.

READ THE PASSAGE Find out what a lemon tree needs.

The Lemon Tree

"Hey! Our tree has tiny lemons on it," Eva said to Alina. "They are hard and green."

"But the leaves don't look very happy," said Alina. "They are droopy and dry."

"You are right," said Eva. "Maybe it isn't getting what it needs. Let's find out how to take care of it."

The girls looked in a book about trees. They found the part about lemon trees. They read that lemon trees like a lot of sun. Lemon trees need to be watered often. When the nights grow cold, lemon trees in pots should be moved into the house. When winter ends, they can be put back outside in a sunny spot. Plant food helps keep the trees healthy.

"Is that the same tree you girls had last winter?" Mother asked one day. "It looks much better than before, and there are so many big yellow lemons."

"Yes, it's the same tree," they said proudly. "We learned how to take care of it."

SKILL PRACTICE Read the question. Fill in the bubble next to the correct answer.

1. As lemons grow, they _____.
   - Ⓐ dry out
   - Ⓑ get droopy
   - Ⓒ get smaller
   - Ⓓ change color

2. To protect a potted tree in the winter, _____.
   - Ⓐ water it every day
   - Ⓑ move it into the house
   - Ⓒ pick its fruit right away
   - Ⓓ give it special plant food

3. To learn how to care for the tree, the girls _____.
   - Ⓐ read a book
   - Ⓑ ask their mother
   - Ⓒ go to a plant store
   - Ⓓ talk to each other

4. Mother notices the tree because _____.
   - Ⓐ it has no lemons on it
   - Ⓑ its leaves are droopy
   - Ⓒ it looks better than before
   - Ⓓ its lemons are hard and green

STRATEGY PRACTICE Tell a partner what the tree looked like at the end of the passage.

READ THE PASSAGE Notice each thing that Chico does.

Smart Thinking

Al and Chico were eating in a Chinese restaurant with their parents. At the end of the meal, the waiter brought fortune cookies. Each one had a piece of paper inside with a message printed on it. "What does your fortune say?" asked Al.

Chico broke open his cookie and pulled out the paper inside it. "It says that I will help others," he said.

The next day at the park, Chico chased a baseball to the corner of the field. There he saw a little dog. It looked lost. Chico knew he had seen the dog before. "That is Ricky's dog, Jesse!" he thought.

Ricky's house was near the park. Chico picked up the dog, carried it to Ricky's house, and knocked on the door. "Jesse!" said Ricky when he opened the door. "Did you dig under the fence again?"

"He was alone in the park," Chico said.

"Thank you for bringing him home!" Ricky said.

"My fortune came true," thought Chico.

SKILL PRACTICE Read the question. Fill in the bubble next to the correct answer.

1. Why does Chico break open his cookie?
   - Ⓐ to share it with Jesse
   - Ⓑ to give a piece of it to Al
   - Ⓒ to save part of it for later
   - Ⓓ to read the message inside of it .

2. Why does Chico run to the corner of the field?
   - Ⓐ He is chasing a ball.
   - Ⓑ A dog is chasing him.
   - Ⓒ He is looking for Ricky's lost dog.
   - Ⓓ He wants to catch up with Ricky.

3. Chico goes to Ricky's house to _____.
   - Ⓐ see Ricky's puppy
   - Ⓑ eat dinner there
   - Ⓒ return Ricky's lost dog
   - Ⓓ pick up his brother

4. Chico's fortune came true because he _____.
   - Ⓐ chased a ball
   - Ⓑ helped Ricky find Jesse
   - Ⓒ went to the park
   - Ⓓ shared his cookie with Al

STRATEGY PRACTICE Retell the story to a partner in the same order the author told it.

Daily Reading Comprehension • EMC 3452 • © Evan-Moor Corp.

Ask yourself how the writer feels about seasons.

Four Great Seasons

Some people live in places where the weather is different each season. Their summers are warm and bright. They go swimming with friends. They have fun hiking, biking, and camping. If they live near water, they can go fishing and boating, too.

People who live in places with four seasons feel summer change to fall. The days grow cool and crisp. As the leaves turn color, the trees look dipped in gold. Children jump into piles of leaves.

People who live in places with four seasons enjoy frosty winters. Their world is often covered with sugar-white snow. They go sledding and build cute snowmen.

People who live in places with four seasons are the most happy when spring comes. People enjoy spending time outdoors after the long, cold winter. Fresh, green leaves appear on the bare trees. Brightly colored flowers bloom.

SKILL PRACTICE   Read the question. Fill in the bubble next to the correct answer.

1. **Which sentence tells that the writer thinks fall trees are pretty?**

   Ⓐ They look dipped in gold.

   Ⓑ They are covered with sugar.

   Ⓒ They are warmed by the sun.

   Ⓓ They turn colors.

2. **Which one is a fact?**

   Ⓐ Camping is fun.

   Ⓑ Winter is too cold.

   Ⓒ Snowmen look cute.

   Ⓓ Fall is after summer.

3. **The writer thinks hiking is _____.**

   Ⓐ silly

   Ⓑ fun

   Ⓒ boring

   Ⓓ dangerous

4. **Which one makes the sentence an opinion?**
   People who have four seasons _____.

   Ⓐ see snow fall in the winter

   Ⓑ are warmest in the summer

   Ⓒ are most happy in the spring

   Ⓓ see leaves change in the fall

STRATEGY PRACTICE   Circle the words that helped you picture each season.

READ THE PASSAGE Look for the writer's opinions.

Cats Are Better

Many people like dogs more than cats. Dogs are friendly and smart. They are fun to spend time with. I think dogs are very nice, but cats make better pets. Cats are quieter. They are cleaner. They are easier to take care of. They are good company, too.

Cats are quiet. They purr softly when they are happy. Cats do not bark loudly like dogs each time someone knocks on the door. They do not bother the neighbors with noises they make. Cats are almost as quiet as mice.

Cats are cleaner than dogs, too. They do not need to be given baths. They clean themselves with their tongues.

Cats are easy to care for. They do not need as much attention as dogs. They do not need daily walks.

Cats are very cozy company. They curl up quietly on their owners' laps.

SKILL PRACTICE Read the question. Fill in the bubble next to the correct answer.

1. The writer thinks dogs are _____.
   Ⓐ cozy
   Ⓑ sleek
   Ⓒ clean
   Ⓓ noisy

2. Which one is an opinion?
   Ⓐ Cats have four legs.
   Ⓑ Cats purr and meow.
   Ⓒ Cats make good pets.
   Ⓓ Cats clean themselves.

3. Which one is a fact?
   Ⓐ Cats do not bark.
   Ⓑ Dogs are too loud.
   Ⓒ Cats make good pets.
   Ⓓ Most people like dogs.

4. The writer thinks cats are _____.
   Ⓐ hard to wash
   Ⓑ easy to care for
   Ⓒ louder than dogs
   Ⓓ quieter than mice

STRATEGY PRACTICE Underline the four main reasons the author gives why cats are better pets than dogs.

READ THE PASSAGE   Pay attention to what happens and why it happens.

Playing with Dirt

"Our yard is not pretty," moaned Sally. "All I see is dirt and more dirt."

Hank scooped some dirt into his hands. "This soil is good, and it has no rocks," said Hank. "It's just right for growing a vegetable garden."

So Sally and Hank shoveled and seeded. They watered and weeded. A few months later, the yard had become a garden of greens.

Green beans on vines twisted up wooden poles. A row of lettuce stood ready to be picked. Their leaves were green ruffles. Strips of cloth tied tomato plants to poles. Ripe tomatoes hung on the stems. They looked like red balls on Christmas trees. Other plants sat in a row. Their leaves were dark green and big. They hid the fat potatoes that grew under the ground.

"Hard work makes dirt look good!" exclaimed Sally.

SKILL PRACTICE   Read the question. Fill in the bubble next to the correct answer.

1. Because Hank and Sally worked hard, _____.
   - Ⓐ they got rid of all the dirt
   - Ⓑ the tomatoes were red
   - Ⓒ they grew a vegetable garden
   - Ⓓ the flowers they grew were pretty

2. The garden grows because _____.
   - Ⓐ Sally does not like the dirt that is in the yard
   - Ⓑ Hank scoops dirt in his hands
   - Ⓒ Sally and Hank tie plants to poles
   - Ⓓ Sally and Hank plant seeds and care for them.

3. Which one states a fact?
   - Ⓐ The soil is rich for growing food.
   - Ⓑ Lettuce leaves are ruffles.
   - Ⓒ The tomatoes look like red balls.
   - Ⓓ Dirt is not pretty.

4. Which one states an opinion?
   - Ⓐ Green beans grow up poles.
   - Ⓑ The yard is not pretty.
   - Ⓒ The dirt has no rocks.
   - Ⓓ Potatoes grow under the ground.

STRATEGY PRACTICE   What is something you pictured about the garden?

_____

Compare and Contrast
Students look for similarities and differences between two or more people or things.

Make Inferences
Students look for clues in the passage and draw upon their own experience to understand information that is not directly stated.

DAY 1

Review the *Compare and Contrast* skill with students. Remind students that when they compare and contrast two or more things, they look for how those things are alike or different. Practice by having students compare and contrast dogs and cats using a Venn diagram (e.g., Both are furry. Both have tails. Dogs bark, but cats meow.). Tell students they are going to read about horses and camels. Then read the instructions at the top of the page aloud. Remind students of the *Ask Questions* strategy, which was taught during Week 5. Say: **As you read the passage, remember questions that you ask yourself about what you read.** Have students read the passage. When students have finished, make a list of questions that they generated during reading. Direct students to complete the strategy practice activity by copying one of the questions. Then direct students to complete the skill practice activity. Review the answers together.

DAY 2

Remind students of the *Compare and Contrast* skill. Read the instructions at the top of the page aloud. Then remind students of the *Monitor Comprehension* strategy, which was taught during Week 6. Draw a Venn diagram on the board, and tell students that using a diagram is a good way to monitor their understanding of how two things are the same or different. Read the passage aloud together. Stop after each paragraph to record information. After completing the Venn diagram, direct students to complete the skill practice activity independently, using the diagram to confirm answers. Review the answers together. For the strategy practice activity, pair students or complete it as a group.

DAY 3

Review the *Make Inferences* skill with students. Say: **When we make an inference, we use clues from the passage and our own experience to figure out information that we haven't been told. If you see people walking toward a field with bats and balls, what can you infer?** (They are going to play baseball.) Remind students of the *Ask Questions* strategy. Tell them that asking questions about the clues that they find in a passage will help them make inferences. Read the instructions at the top of the page aloud. Then direct students to read the passage and to complete the skill practice activity. Review the answers together. For the strategy practice activity, give students time to write their questions individually, and then pair students to share their questions with a partner.

DAY 4

Remind students of the *Make Inferences* skill—and that frequently a passage will give you facts you can use as clues to arrive at a conclusion about the topic. Read the instructions at the top of the page aloud. Remind students of the *Monitor Comprehension* strategy. Mention to students that as they read, they should pause to make sure they are understanding what is being said about the rooster. If they don't remember, they should reread. Direct students to read the passage and to complete the skill practice activity. Review the answers together. For the strategy practice activity, pair students or complete it together.

DAY 5

Tell students they will practice both the *Compare and Contrast* and *Make Inferences* skills. Read the instructions at the top of the page aloud. Direct students to read the passage and to complete the skill practice activity. Review the answers together. For the strategy practice activity, remind students of the *Ask Questions* strategy—that one way to find out if you understood what you read is to think of questions to ask about the information. Give students time to write their questions individually, and then pair students to share their questions with a partner.

Daily Reading Comprehension • EMC 3452 • © Evan-Moor Corp.

READ THE PASSAGE Find out how horses and camels are alike and different.

Which Ride Is for You?

You're going camping in a far-off desert campground. You can't get there by car. There are no roads, only trails. You can ride a horse or you can ride a camel! Which one will you choose? Here are some facts to help you decide.

Camels are a lot taller than most horses. A camel must kneel down for you to get on. But you can see a lot from way up there! Camels don't wear iron shoes like horses do. Their feet make little noise. You can easily hear the birds singing and the guide pointing out interesting sights. Horses' feet clippity-clop noisily as they walk.

Horses are faster than camels. They are more sure-footed on rough, rocky trails, too. But camels are more sensible. They don't get frightened as easily as horses. If a horse gets its feet tangled in a rope, it may panic and hurt itself. A camel is more likely to stop and figure out what to do.

Both horses and camels can travel long distances and go over 20 miles a day. But camels can go many days without food and water. Horses need food and water every day.

Which animal would you choose?

SKILL PRACTICE Read the question. Fill in the bubble next to the correct answer.

1. Horses and camels both _____.
   - Ⓐ need water every day
   - Ⓑ wear shoes
   - Ⓒ carry people
   - Ⓓ have humps

2. Horses and camels both _____.
   - Ⓐ kneel down for the rider
   - Ⓑ can go long distances
   - Ⓒ get frightened easily
   - Ⓓ make a lot of noise when they walk

3. Horses are _____ than camels.
   - Ⓐ faster
   - Ⓑ bigger
   - Ⓒ quieter
   - Ⓓ stronger

4. Camels _____ than horses.
   - Ⓐ are more sure-footed
   - Ⓑ need more water
   - Ⓒ make more noise
   - Ⓓ are less likely to be frightened

STRATEGY PRACTICE Write a question you asked yourself as you read the passage.

_____

READ THE PASSAGE Think about which kind of skiing seems more fun.

Ready to Ski

Snow skiers glide down bright white hills. Then they ride ski lifts back to the top. Most skiers ski on two skis. They wear boots and gloves. They wear jackets and hats to stay warm in the frosty weather. Snow skiers hold a pole in each hand. The poles help them balance and turn.

Water-skiers slide over the water. They hold onto towropes. They are pulled behind motorboats and make turns on the water. Some use two skis. Others use just one. Some water-skiers are called "barefooters." They use no skis at all!

Water-skiers wear bathing suits. When the water is cold, they wear wet suits to stay warm. They wear life jackets for safety, too.

Some water-skiers and snow skiers like to do fancy tricks. They ski over jumps and do flips in the air. Wow! They are fun to watch.

SKILL PRACTICE Read the question. Fill in the bubble next to the correct answer.

1. All of the skiers in the passage _____.
   Ⓐ slide and glide for fun
   Ⓑ flip in the air
   Ⓒ hold towropes
   Ⓓ wear life jackets

2. Snow skiers are different from water-skiers because of _____.
   Ⓐ the reason they ski
   Ⓑ the places they ski
   Ⓒ how well they ski
   Ⓓ how much they ski

3. Water-skiers and most snow skiers _____.
   Ⓐ ride ski lifts
   Ⓑ wear hats
   Ⓒ make turns
   Ⓓ wear wet suits

4. Both kinds of skiers _____.
   Ⓐ carry two poles
   Ⓑ can go barefoot
   Ⓒ ski behind boats
   Ⓓ can do fancy tricks

STRATEGY PRACTICE Tell a partner two facts about snow skiing and two facts about water-skiing.

Picture what the tent trailer must be like.

A Tent with Wheels

My family went on a road trip last summer. We pulled a tent trailer behind our car. We stopped at a different camp every night. When we reached a camp, we first hopped out of the car. Then we unfolded the trailer. It opened quickly and easily. It is like a tiny home!

In the middle of the trailer is a sink. Beside it is a little stove. We sat outside on lawn chairs to eat the soup or eggs Mom made.

Bedtimes were cozy. We put out the campfire. Then we washed up in the sink and went to bed. My sister and I shared a bed on one side of the trailer. Our parents slept in the bed on the other side. We were snug while the wind whistled through the trees outside.

As we pulled out of the camp the next morning, the trailer looked like a big, flat box. It was hard to believe that it was a tiny home at night.

SKILL PRACTICE Read the question. Fill in the bubble next to the correct answer.

1. **Where did Mom probably cook the meals?**
   Ⓐ on a barbecue
   Ⓑ over a campfire
   Ⓒ at home before the trip
   Ⓓ on the stove in the trailer

2. **Who probably unfolded the trailer?**
   Ⓐ the writer's parents
   Ⓑ the writer and her family
   Ⓒ the workers at the camp
   Ⓓ the writer's father and sister

3. **How do you think the writer feels at bedtime in the trailer?**
   Ⓐ cold
   Ⓑ homesick
   Ⓒ safe
   Ⓓ scared

4. **Before they left each camp, the family likely _____.**
   Ⓐ folded up the trailer
   Ⓑ walked to another camp
   Ⓒ wished they were home
   Ⓓ packed the boxes

STRATEGY PRACTICE Write a question about tent trailers that can be answered by information in the passage. Have a partner answer your question.

READ THE PASSAGE   Look for clues that tell you how the people feel about the rooster.

Time to Wake Up

Some children set alarm clocks each night. Their clocks buzz or play music in the morning. I wake up to a loud cock-a-doodle-doo! My rooster, Rick, crows when he sees the sun peek over the hill.

Rick is very handsome and proud. Rick protects the hens on our farm. He stands in the tree as a lookout. If Rick sees a fox moving toward the hens, he crows at the top of his lungs. Dad runs to make sure the hens are safe. "Thanks for your help, Rick," he says.

Sometimes Rick crows in the middle of the night. Then I think it's time to get up. Once, I was all dressed for school when I realized that it was not morning yet! I smiled and put my pajamas back on. Then I snuggled back into bed.

SKILL PRACTICE   Read the question. Fill in the bubble next to the correct answer.

1. Why do you think some children set alarm clocks?

   Ⓐ They do not want to be late.

   Ⓑ They want to see the foxes.

   Ⓒ They want to feed their roosters.

   Ⓓ They do not want to miss sunrise.

2. What do most people probably do when their alarm clocks go off?

   Ⓐ get into bed

   Ⓑ get out of bed

   Ⓒ check on their hens

   Ⓓ put on their pajamas

3. The author probably does not need an alarm clock because _____.

   Ⓐ the hens wake him up

   Ⓑ the sun wakes him up

   Ⓒ his father wakes him up

   Ⓓ his rooster wakes him up

4. When Rick wakes the author too early one day, the author most likely _____.

   Ⓐ is angry

   Ⓑ yells at Rick

   Ⓒ thinks it's funny

   Ⓓ feels bothered

STRATEGY PRACTICE   In three sentences or less, describe Rick to a partner.

READ THE PASSAGE Remember what the children do and feel on the way to school.

Off to School

Most of my friends walk to school each day, but I like to ride my bike. After I eat breakfast and wash up for school, I throw on my backpack. Do I have my lunch? Do I have my books and homework? Yes, I do.

I take my bike from the garage. I hop onto my bike and sail down the driveway. "See you later, Mom," I say.

I pass my friends as I ride by. "Hi, Matt!" they call as I pass. Marta does not want to ride with me. She does not like to wear a backpack. She likes to carry her books in her arms as she walks. She likes to look at flowers in the yards. She likes to pet cats on doorsteps. She likes to kick the fall leaves.

Not me! I like to fly on my bike with the fresh air in my face. When I get to school, I lock my bike in a rack. I walk across the field to say hi to Mrs. Brown and wait for my friends in our classroom.

SKILL PRACTICE Read the question. Fill in the bubble next to the correct answer.

1. All of the children in the passage _____.
   Ⓐ kick fall leaves
   Ⓑ wear backpacks
   Ⓒ are riding bicycles
   Ⓓ are going to school

2. The children who walk are probably <u>not</u> carrying _____.
   Ⓐ locks
   Ⓑ lunch bags
   Ⓒ homework
   Ⓓ schoolbooks

3. The writer and Marta both _____.
   Ⓐ enjoy petting cats
   Ⓑ enjoy the trip to school
   Ⓒ like to look at flowers in yards
   Ⓓ like to feel the air in their faces

4. One way the writer is different from Marta is that he _____.
   Ⓐ kicks the leaves
   Ⓑ carries his books in his arms
   Ⓒ wears a backpack
   Ⓓ pets cats on the way to school

STRATEGY PRACTICE Write a question you have about the passage. Have a partner answer it.

Character and Setting
Students study a passage to better understand who or what is at the center of the action and when and where the action takes place.

Fantasy and Reality
Students identify which things in the passage could or could not happen in real life.

DAY 1

Review the *Character and Setting* skill with students. Then say: **The characters are who a story or passage is mostly about. The setting is where and when a story or passage takes place.** Tell students they are going to read a story about firefighters. Read the instructions at the top of the page aloud. Then remind students of the *Make Connections* strategy, which was taught during Week 1. Say: **It is easier to understand what the characters do when you think about what you know about firefighters.** Direct students to read the passage and to complete the skill practice activity. Review the answers together. For the strategy practice activity, pair students or complete it as a group.

DAY 2

Remind students of the *Character and Setting* skill. Tell students they are going to read about an accident during a soccer game. Read the instructions at the top of the page aloud. Then remind students of the *Visualization* strategy, which was taught during Week 2. Say: **Making a mental picture of the characters and setting will help you understand and remember what you read.** Direct students to read the passage and to complete the skill practice activity. Review the answers together. Complete the strategy practice activity as a group. Point out that descriptive words are some of the words that help us form vivid mental pictures.

DAY 3

Review the *Fantasy and Reality* skill with students. Say: **When something happens in a story that could happen or exist in real life, it is reality. Things that could not happen or exist in real life are fantasy.** Read the instructions at the top of the page aloud, and point out that there must be something in the story that is fantasy. Then remind students of the *Make Connections* strategy. Say: **We can tell what is not real by using our own experiences and knowledge of the world to compare with the things that happen in the story.** Have students read the passage. Then discuss what similarities to other fantasy stories students noticed. Direct students to complete the skill practice activity, and review the answers together. For the strategy practice activity, pair students or complete it as a group.

DAY 4

Remind students of the *Fantasy and Reality* skill. Read the instructions at the top of the page aloud. Then read the title of the passage. Remind students to use *Visualization* to help them form clear ideas about what is happening and what can and cannot happen. Direct students to read the passage and to complete the skill practice activity. Review the answers together. For the strategy practice activity, pair students or complete it as a group.

DAY 5

Tell students they will practice both the *Character and Setting* and *Fantasy and Reality* skills. Review the skills if necessary, and then read the instructions at the top of the page aloud. Remind students to use their own experiences and knowledge of the world to make connections between themselves and the characters and events in the story. Have students read the passage. When students have finished, direct them to complete the skill practice activity. Review the answers together. For the strategy practice activity, pair students or complete it as a group.

READ THE PASSAGE Pay attention to how the characters act.

Firefighters on Duty

The bell rang at the station. The firefighters leaped up. They pulled on their boots and helmets. They leaped into the big red truck. Cars on the street moved out of the way as the truck with a screaming siren rushed by. The firefighters were going to a big building that was on fire.

"Are there people inside?" one firefighter asked the captain on their way to the fire.

"I don't know," the captain said. "We'll have to check." When the firefighters got to the building, the captain ran once around the building. Another firefighter began to unroll the heavy hoses. When the captain came back, he called for more help.

"This is a big fire," the captain said. "Send more trucks."

Two firefighters ran into the building. Smoke and flames were everywhere. Thankfully, no one was inside. The firefighters ran out of the building.

Soon, more trucks showed up. The trucks were full of water. All of the firefighters sprayed the building with water from the trucks. It took a long time, but they put out the fire. Then the firefighters went back to the station.

SKILL PRACTICE Read the question. Fill in the bubble next to the correct answer.

1. The firefighters in the passage _____.
   Ⓐ get ready slowly
   Ⓑ care about people
   Ⓒ drive the truck badly
   Ⓓ only want to fight fires

2. When the bell rings, the firefighters are _____.
   Ⓐ at the station
   Ⓑ fighting a fire
   Ⓒ driving their truck
   Ⓓ in someone's home

3. Most of the passage takes place _____.
   Ⓐ at the fire station
   Ⓑ in the firetruck
   Ⓒ at a big building
   Ⓓ beside a water truck

4. The firefighters in the passage _____.
   Ⓐ want to eat their lunch
   Ⓑ are afraid of the fire
   Ⓒ work hard to put out the fire
   Ⓓ do not listen to the captain

STRATEGY PRACTICE Tell a partner what you know about firefighters.

READ THE PASSAGE Notice how the characters act toward Kevin.

Broken Arm

Kevin was playing soccer at the park. His team was doing great, and Kevin was kicking the ball toward the goal. Suddenly, he tripped over the ball and fell sideways onto the field. Ouch! Kevin landed on his arm. It hurt badly.

Coach ran over to Kevin on the field. "Hang in there, Kevin. I know it hurts. We'll get you to a doctor." Kevin's parents ran onto the field. The players on both teams clapped as Kevin's father helped him walk to the car.

The hospital was big, clean, and shiny. The people there were nice. They took a picture of Kevin's arm. Then the doctor told Kevin that there was a crack in one of the bones. He put a big white cast on Kevin's arm. He gave him a marker, too. Kevin's parents were the first ones to write on his cast. His friends would write on it later.

SKILL PRACTICE Read the question. Fill in the bubble next to the correct answer.

1. Where is Kevin when he gets hurt?
   Ⓐ at a park
   Ⓑ on his street
   Ⓒ at his school
   Ⓓ in a backyard

2. Which word describes the coach?
   Ⓐ mean
   Ⓑ understanding
   Ⓒ loud
   Ⓓ angry

3. What does the doctor do that is kind?
   Ⓐ He tells Kevin his arm is broken.
   Ⓑ He writes on Kevin's cast.
   Ⓒ He takes a picture of Kevin's arm.
   Ⓓ He gives Kevin a marker so people can write on his cast.

4. Which word describes the hospital?
   Ⓐ dirty
   Ⓑ scary
   Ⓒ clean
   Ⓓ gloomy

STRATEGY PRACTICE Underline words in the story that help you picture the characters and the setting.

READ THE PASSAGE Notice what in the passage is fantasy.

Upside-Down World

Darcy and Eva were lying with their heads upside down over the edge of the bed. They were looking through the big window near the bed. The window went all the way down to the floor. When the girls looked through the window upside down, everything looked different. A tree grew "down" toward the sky. The sky looked like a huge blue pool.

"I wish I could climb down to those branches," Darcy said.

"Me, too," Eva said. Suddenly, she floated through the window. She held on to the trunk of the tree. "Wow!" said Eva. "Let's go!" She slid down to the top of the tree.

"Whee!" said Darcy as she swung from a branch. Her feet hung over the sky. "Watch this!" she said. She sailed through the air and landed on top of a streetlight. Darcy swung her legs as she sat on the top of the light. "Let's fly down to those white, puffy clouds!" The girls put their arms out like wings. Poof! They landed on a soft cloud.

"Yum! This cloud tastes like whipped cream," Eva said.

SKILL PRACTICE Read the question. Fill in the bubble next to the correct answer.

1. **Where does the passage begin?**
   Ⓐ in a tree
   Ⓑ on a bed
   Ⓒ in a pool
   Ⓓ on a cloud

2. **Which one could really happen?**
   Ⓐ sliding down to the top of a tree
   Ⓑ landing on a cloud
   Ⓒ floating through the window
   Ⓓ swinging from a branch

3. **Which one is make-believe?**
   Ⓐ a window that goes to the floor
   Ⓑ playing a fun game
   Ⓒ tasting a cloud
   Ⓓ looking through a window

4. **The passage stops being real when _____.**
   Ⓐ Eva floats through the window
   Ⓑ Eva slides down to the treetop
   Ⓒ Darcy sits on a streetlight
   Ⓓ Darcy hangs her feet over the sky

STRATEGY PRACTICE Tell a partner about an imaginary game you have played.

READ THE PASSAGE   Notice where the story becomes fantasy.

Part of the Show

"I love this part of the movie," Gabe said. "I always want to be in it."

"Me, too!" said his brother Sam. "We would be cowboys." The boys were in their living room. The next moment, they were inside the TV! Gabe was riding a horse and had a long rope in one hand.

"Wow! You look good in a cowboy hat, Sam. Watch me lasso that cow!" Gabe swung his rope in a circle in the air. Then he threw the loop over a cow's head. "How did I do that?" Gabe asked.

"You are in a cowboy movie!" Sam said. "That cow was running away from the herd. I'll bet it would have gotten lost if you hadn't caught it with your rope."

The boys rode after the herd for a while. They felt like real cowboys. Then they saw some riders in black hats on the top of a nearby hill.

"Oh, no. It's the bad guys," Gabe said. "Let's go home." And the boys jumped back into their living room.

SKILL PRACTICE   Read the question. Fill in the bubble next to the correct answer.

1. The passage is about two boys who _____.
   - Ⓐ ride horses in a rodeo
   - Ⓑ become part of a movie
   - Ⓒ learn to take care of cows
   - Ⓓ wear cowboy hats

2. Which one is make-believe?
   - Ⓐ roping a cow
   - Ⓑ riding a horse
   - Ⓒ going inside a TV
   - Ⓓ acting in a Western movie

3. Which one could be real?
   - Ⓐ a rope appearing in your hand
   - Ⓑ jumping through the TV
   - Ⓒ a horse appearing under you
   - Ⓓ wanting to be a cowboy

4. The story stops being real when the boys _____.
   - Ⓐ leave their living room
   - Ⓑ have fun riding horses
   - Ⓒ jump back into their home
   - Ⓓ see bad guys on the hill

STRATEGY PRACTICE   Share what you saw in your mind with a partner.

READ THE PASSAGE Think about why the writer used fantasy in the passage.

Tito Cares

"Please give me some nuts!" screeched the monkey. Tito jumped and stared.

"What's wrong?" asked the monkey. "You look scared."

"It scares me that you talk like a person," Tito said.

"Don't be afraid," said the monkey. "Only good people can hear me."

"I can't believe it," Tito thought to himself as he walked away from the monkey cage. He went to see the tigers next.

"Hey," said the biggest tiger as it stretched. "What's a cool cat like you doing here?"

"Losing my mind, I guess," said Tito. "Animals are talking to me."

"You are finding your mind, not losing it," laughed the tiger. "We only talk to people who understand. We talk to people who care." The tiger winked at Tito.

"I do care about animals," said Tito, "but what good does that do?"

"There are many things you can do to protect us," said the tiger. "We depend on you."

SKILL PRACTICE Read the question. Fill in the bubble next to the correct answer.

1. Where does the passage take place?
    Ⓐ in a zoo
    Ⓑ in a jungle
    Ⓒ at a circus
    Ⓓ at a pet store

2. Which word describes Tito?
    Ⓐ silly
    Ⓑ tired
    Ⓒ careless
    Ⓓ surprised

3. Which one is make-believe?
    Ⓐ a boy who looks at animals
    Ⓑ a tiger in the zoo
    Ⓒ animals that talk like people
    Ⓓ a monkey that eats nuts

4. Which one could really happen?
    Ⓐ A tiger laughs.
    Ⓑ A tiger stretches.
    Ⓒ A tiger winks at a boy.
    Ⓓ A tiger talks like a person.

STRATEGY PRACTICE Discuss with a partner animals that need protection.

Author's Purpose
Students think about why an author wrote a particular passage.

Prediction
Students use clues from the text and their own background knowledge to anticipate what is likely to happen next or what information will come next.

DAY 1

Review the *Author's Purpose* skill with students, and remind them of the common purposes for writing something: to give information, to entertain, to tell how to do something, or to persuade. Also remind students of the *Ask Questions* strategy, which was taught during Week 5. Say: **As you read, stop after each paragraph and ask yourself,** *What is the purpose of this paragraph? What are the important ideas?* Read the title aloud. Then read the instructions at the top of the page aloud. Help students conclude that a *cavern* is a cave. Then have students read the passage. Discuss the author's purpose (to give information; to describe an interesting place). Direct students to complete the skill practice activity, and review the answers together. Complete the strategy practice activity together.

DAY 2

Remind students of the *Author's Purpose* skill, and review the most common purposes: to give information, to tell a story that entertains, to tell how to do something, and to persuade. Then remind students of the *Make Connections* strategy, which was taught during Week 1. Say: **When authors write, they often want to make a connection with the reader. As you think about the author's purpose, look for places where the author tries to make a connection with you.** Read the instructions at the top of the page aloud. Then direct students to read the passage and to complete the skill practice activity. For the strategy practice activity, pair students or complete it as a group.

DAY 3

Review the *Prediction* skill with students. Say: **When we predict, we use information from the passage and our own experiences to make a good guess about what is likely to happen next.** Then remind students of the *Ask Questions* strategy. Say: **As you read, you can ask questions about what you have read to make sure you understand what is happening and to make sure you don't miss important clues in the passage that help you make a prediction.** Tell students they are going to read about a girl who is snow skiing with her dad. If necessary, explain skiing terminology and perhaps show students photos of chair lifts. Read the instructions at the top of the page aloud. Direct students to read the passage and to complete the skill practice activity. Review the answers together. For the strategy practice activity, pair students or complete it as a group.

DAY 4

Remind students of both the *Prediction* skill and the *Make Connections* strategy. Say: **By making connections, you use past experiences to help you understand what you read. These connections also help you make predictions.** Read the instructions at the top of the page aloud. Direct students to read the passage and to complete the activities. Review the answers together. Invite students to share their strategy practice activity responses.

DAY 5

Tell students they will practice both the *Author's Purpose* and *Prediction* skills. If necessary, review the definitions of each skill. Then read the instructions at the top of the page aloud. Remind students of the *Ask Questions* strategy. Say: **As you read, you will also want to ask yourself questions about what the author wants you to understand.** Have students read the passage. When students have finished, direct them to complete the skill practice activity. Then review the answers together. Direct students to complete the strategy practice activity independently, and then invite students to share their responses.

READ THE PASSAGE Ask yourself, "Why did the author write the passage?"

Fantastic Caverns

Do you want to see something really cool? Go to Fantastic Caverns! It is an underground cave in the state of Missouri. There are many caverns in North America. But this is the only one with a cave wide enough to drive through. To see the inside of the cave, visitors ride in open cars pulled by a jeep.

Down they go. They ooh and ah. The cave is very beautiful! It is filled with shapes that have been formed by water. Minerals in the water have formed rock towers that grow up from the cave floor. Other shapes hang down from the ceiling of the cave. These shapes are strange and wonderful. This cave feels like a magical place.

There is no natural light in the cave. Different kinds of cave fish live in the dark water. Bats fly through the dark air. They are very clever. They do not need light.

Who do you suppose found this hidden cave? A farmer's dog! Imagine how surprised the townspeople were. The cave had been beneath them all along.

SKILL PRACTICE Read the question. Fill in the bubble next to the correct answer.

1. According to the author, Fantastic Caverns is a good place to _____.

    Ⓐ live

    Ⓑ fish

    Ⓒ camp

    Ⓓ visit

2. The author thinks bats are _____.

    Ⓐ scary

    Ⓑ clever

    Ⓒ magic

    Ⓓ lonely

3. The author says this cave is _____.

    Ⓐ wider than many others

    Ⓑ more hidden than others

    Ⓒ darker than many others

    Ⓓ more magical than others

4. The author wrote the passage to _____.

    Ⓐ tell you a make-believe story

    Ⓑ scare you into staying above ground

    Ⓒ tell you about a special cavern

    Ⓓ let you know about a farmer's dog

STRATEGY PRACTICE What is the author's purpose in the second paragraph?

_____

READ THE PASSAGE   Remember the ways the author says we use math every day.

Math Matters

Who cares about times tables? Why do we have to learn math? You may feel that math is not important. It does matter, though. We use it every day.

Imagine going to buy an ice-cream cone. You look at the coins you have. You must add the value of each coin to the others. Do you have enough to buy a cone? If so, how much change should you get back? You are using math.

Say you are playing kickball. You use math to tally the score. You use math to form the teams, too. You take the number of players and divide that number by two.

When you grow up, you will use math even more. Grown-ups use math for banking. They use it for shopping and traveling. Math matters a lot. You'll see!

SKILL PRACTICE   Read the question. Fill in the bubble next to the correct answer.

1. The author thinks math is _____.
   - Ⓐ very useful
   - Ⓑ very confusing
   - Ⓒ only used by children
   - Ⓓ only used to keep score

2. The author says we use math _____.
   - Ⓐ once a week
   - Ⓑ every day
   - Ⓒ once a year
   - Ⓓ once a month

3. The author thinks that some children do <u>not</u> _____.
   - Ⓐ think math is important
   - Ⓑ like to eat ice-cream cones
   - Ⓒ like to have money in their pockets
   - Ⓓ like to play games with their friends

4. The author says grown-ups _____.
   - Ⓐ use math a lot
   - Ⓑ think math is just for children
   - Ⓒ need to learn more math
   - Ⓓ only use math for shopping

STRATEGY PRACTICE   Discuss with a partner how each of you uses math every day.

READ THE PASSAGE Notice how Hannah's feelings change.

The Big Hill

Hannah stood at the top of the hill. The bottom looked very far away. She felt a little afraid, but ready. She would ski down the big hill today.

"All set, Hannah?" Dad asked. "Are you sure you want to do this?"

"Yes, I am," Hannah said loudly. She remembered how she had gotten scared last time. She rode the chair lift back down to the bottom. Dad said it was OK, but she felt bad.

The lodge below looked like a toy. Hannah thought about the hot chocolate that was sold there. She liked to sit by the fire with her ski boots off and warm her toes.

The first turn was the hardest. After that, it became easier. "Nice turn!" called Dad. "I'm right here. Follow me. Turn where I do."

Hannah followed Dad. The lodge grew closer and closer. When they were near the bottom, Hannah smiled. "Now you follow me!" she said.

SKILL PRACTICE Read the question. Fill in the bubble next to the correct answer.

1. **What do you think Dad will do next?**
   Ⓐ follow Hannah
   Ⓑ take off his skis
   Ⓒ go ahead of Hannah
   Ⓓ ride the chair lift to the bottom

2. **What do you think Hannah will want when they get to the lodge?**
   Ⓐ a hot dog
   Ⓑ warm soup
   Ⓒ a hamburger
   Ⓓ hot chocolate

3. **What will Hannah probably do when she sits by the fire?**
   Ⓐ tell Dad she wants to go home
   Ⓑ take off her boots
   Ⓒ sign up for a lesson
   Ⓓ choose a new sport

4. **What might happen the next time Hannah goes to the top of the hill?**
   Ⓐ She will fall down the hill.
   Ⓑ She will forget how to ski.
   Ⓒ She will feel less afraid.
   Ⓓ She will ride the chair lift down.

STRATEGY PRACTICE Ask a partner some questions about the passage that begin with *Why*.

READ THE PASSAGE Think about what Evan should do.

The Book Report

Evan knew he should have been working on his book report. He had to draw a picture of part of the book they were reading in class. Evan was going to draw the town where the family in the book lives. He would draw little streets, the store, the post office, and the school. In the middle of the picture, he would draw the family's house with their dog, Rusty, beside it.

The picture was due on Friday. Friday? That was tomorrow! How had it come so fast? Evan kept meaning to work on the picture, but other things got in the way. His dog wanted to go for a walk. His friends asked him to play ball.

This was his last day to work on the picture. Evan put a piece of paper on the table. He put some colored pencils beside it. He wondered if there were any good shows on TV!

SKILL PRACTICE Read the question. Fill in the bubble next to the correct answer.

1. What will Evan probably do next?
   - Ⓐ turn on the TV
   - Ⓑ finish his book report
   - Ⓒ take his dog for a walk
   - Ⓓ get a snack

2. What is likely to happen at school on Friday?
   - Ⓐ Evan will surprise his teacher.
   - Ⓑ Evan will go home sick.
   - Ⓒ Evan will not have a book report.
   - Ⓓ Evan's teacher will be happy.

3. Evan had a plan, but he probably _____.
   - Ⓐ decided it was not a good one
   - Ⓑ had a hard time completing it
   - Ⓒ let his friends talk him out of it
   - Ⓓ did not have paper and pencils

4. If Evan learns a lesson, next time he will probably _____.
   - Ⓐ not care about the book report
   - Ⓑ do the book report right away
   - Ⓒ buy new colored pencils
   - Ⓓ ask his friends to do his book report

STRATEGY PRACTICE Write about a time when you waited to do something important.

_____

_____

READ THE PASSAGE Ask yourself what the author wants you to know.

Sea Turtles

What could be cuter than a baby sea turtle? It would fit in the palm of your hand. You can see sea turtles on Anna Maria Island in Florida. The turtles are protected there.

Summer visitors can go on special walks. They go early in the morning. Guides lead visitors to a beach where the turtles lay their eggs. The walkers must be very quiet. They must not scare the turtles!

Sea turtles travel hundreds of miles to lay their eggs. They go back to the same beach each year. Each one lays 70 to 150 eggs! The eggs are small, round, and white. They look like ping-pong balls. Two months later, the babies will hatch. Then they will crawl to the water. They will ride ocean currents east to a part of the Atlantic Ocean with lots of seaweed. They will float safely and grow there.

SKILL PRACTICE Read the question. Fill in the bubble next to the correct answer.

1. The author thinks baby sea turtles look _____.
   - Ⓐ ugly
   - Ⓑ cute
   - Ⓒ round
   - Ⓓ white

2. If visitors scared the turtles, the turtles might _____.
   - Ⓐ lose the eggs
   - Ⓑ bite the visitors
   - Ⓒ not lay eggs
   - Ⓓ go to a new beach

3. What will the turtles likely do after they grow up?
   - Ⓐ go back to where they hatched
   - Ⓑ swim farther west
   - Ⓒ stay in the seaweed
   - Ⓓ find a new beach to live

4. The author wants you to _____.
   - Ⓐ learn about ping-pong balls
   - Ⓑ know how to be quiet
   - Ⓒ know where seaweed grows
   - Ⓓ learn about sea turtles

STRATEGY PRACTICE Write a question about sea turtles that you thought of while you were reading.

_____

Nonfiction Text Features

Students look at text features, such as headings and captions, to better understand what they read.

Visual Information

Students discover how pictures, charts, graphs, and other visual elements can explain more about a topic.

DAY 1

Remind students that nonfiction text features are related to the main body of text in a passage but different from it. Invite a volunteer to read the title of the passage. Then read the instructions at the top of the page aloud. Remind students of the *Determine Important Information* strategy, which was taught during Week 4. Say: **As you read, think about why each piece of information is included. Think about who would need to know that information.** Read the schedule aloud as a class, calling on individuals to read various sections, and pointing out the headings as nonfiction text features. Direct students to complete the skill and strategy practice activities. Review the answers together.

DAY 2

Remind students of the *Nonfiction Text Features* skill. Then remind them of the *Organization* strategy, which was taught during Week 3. Say: **Nonfiction text features can be organized in a way to make information easier to find.** Read the instructions at the top of the page aloud. Ask students to look at the information and determine what kind of information it is (an explanation of what goes in each waste container). Read the information aloud together, calling students' attention to the bold and boxed headings. Discuss what information the headings give. Direct students to complete the skill and strategy practice activities. Review the answers together. Then compile a list of students' responses to the strategy practice activity.

DAY 3

Remind students that visual information can be given as pictures, graphs, charts, and maps, and that sometimes visual information is easier and quicker to understand than text. Tell students they are going to study an invitation to a birthday party and that some of the information is given as visual information. Remind students of the *Determine Important Information* strategy. Read the instructions at the top of the page aloud. Ask volunteers to read parts of the invitation. As each part is read, decide as a group if that information is the most important. Direct students to complete the skill and strategy practice activities independently. Review the answers together.

DAY 4

Review that *visual information* is the term for non-word features such as pictures, maps, and charts. Ask students to look at the passage to see if they recognize anything from it. Allow time for students to share their observations. Remind students of the *Organization* strategy. Say: **Scientific information must be shown in a particular way or it is not correct.** Guide students through the solar system illustration, having volunteers read the text and the names of the planets in order. Discuss the reasons why the sizes and distances from each other vary (Planets are different sizes. The distances between planets is not the same.). Direct students to complete the skill practice activity, and then review the answers together. Complete the strategy practice activity together, guiding students to express the idea that in order to be correct, the illustration must show the planets in the order they are arranged in space.

DAY 5

Tell students that they will practice both the *Nonfiction Text Features* and *Visual Information* skills. Remind students of the *Determine Important Information* strategy. Say: **Studying nonfiction text features and visual information will help you determine which information is important.** Read the instructions at the top of the page aloud. Then guide students through the information. Direct students to complete the activities independently. Review the answers together, allowing students to share responses to the strategy practice activity item and give reasons for their choices.

Daily Reading Comprehension • EMC 3452 • © Evan-Moor Corp.

READ THE SCHEDULE Look for information that the players need to know.

THE TIGERS
Soccer Team Snack Schedule

On your assigned day, please bring water or juice and a healthy snack to share with your teammates. Tell Coach Lugo if you need to switch your snack date with another player.

Game Date	Game Time	Name of Player
September 13	10:00	Ava
September 20	10:00	Correy
September 27	9:00	Emma
October 4	1:00	Haley
October 11	4:00	Jada
October 18	11:00	Jessie
October 25	10:00	Maria
November 1	12:00	Rayann
November 8	9:00	Toni
November 15	9:00	Ava

November 21 — Team Party — Noon at Pete's Pizza Palace!

SKILL PRACTICE Read the question. Fill in the bubble next to the correct answer.

1. What does the schedule show?
   Ⓐ which teams will be playing
   Ⓑ where each game will be played
   Ⓒ what kinds of snacks are healthy
   Ⓓ who will bring snacks to each game

2. The times in the middle column tell when _____.
   Ⓐ games end
   Ⓑ games begin
   Ⓒ players should arrive
   Ⓓ snacks will be served

3. Who will be bringing a snack twice?
   Ⓐ Ava
   Ⓑ Jada
   Ⓒ Maria
   Ⓓ Emma

4. What happens on November 21?
   Ⓐ The coach has a birthday.
   Ⓑ The team gets new uniforms.
   Ⓒ The team has a party.
   Ⓓ Ava brings the last snack.

STRATEGY PRACTICE Write the headings from the schedule.

READ THE INFORMATION Notice how the information is put into groups.

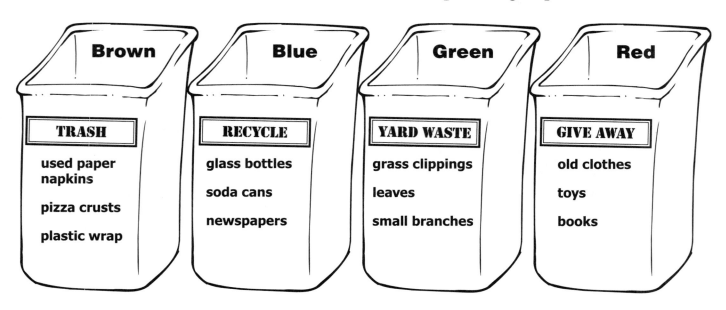

Brown | **Blue** | **Green** | **Red**

| TRASH | RECYCLE | YARD WASTE | GIVE AWAY |

TRASH
used paper napkins

pizza crusts

plastic wrap

RECYCLE
glass bottles

soda cans

newspapers

YARD WASTE
grass clippings

leaves

small branches

GIVE AWAY
old clothes

toys

books

SKILL PRACTICE Read the question. Fill in the bubble next to the correct answer.

1. The bold word at the top of each container tells the color of the _____.

   Ⓐ container

   Ⓑ leaves

   Ⓒ bottles

   Ⓓ napkins

2. What do the words in all capital letters tell?

   Ⓐ where to buy the containers

   Ⓑ who to call with questions

   Ⓒ why the containers are different

   Ⓓ what kind of item goes in each container

3. Leaves would go into the _____.

   Ⓐ red container

   Ⓑ blue container

   Ⓒ green container

   Ⓓ brown container

4. Into which container would a glass soda bottle go?

   Ⓐ TRASH

   Ⓑ RECYCLE

   Ⓒ GIVE AWAY

   Ⓓ YARD WASTE

STRATEGY PRACTICE What is another thing that could be listed on the red container?

_____

Name: _____

READ THE INFORMATION   Think about how the pictures help the reader.

SKILL PRACTICE   Read the question. Fill in the bubble next to the correct answer.

1. The information above is _____.

   Ⓐ a menu

   Ⓑ an invitation

   Ⓒ a shopping list

   Ⓓ a yard sale sign

2. Casey's house is _____.

   Ⓐ in a park

   Ⓑ on a corner

   Ⓒ on Main Street

   Ⓓ at the end of the street

3. What will you eat at the party?

   Ⓐ ice cream

   Ⓑ pancakes

   Ⓒ hot dogs

   Ⓓ tacos

4. Where will you sleep at the party?

   Ⓐ on bunk beds

   Ⓑ on the TV room floor

   Ⓒ in a tent

   Ⓓ in a cabin

STRATEGY PRACTICE   If you were Casey's neighbor, what information would you **not** need to know?

_____

READ THE PASSAGE Think about how the information is arranged.

Our Solar System

Our solar system is made up of the sun and the planets that go around it. Some of the planets are smaller than Earth. Some of the planets are larger than Earth.

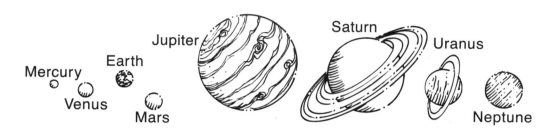

SKILL PRACTICE Read the question. Fill in the bubble next to the correct answer.

1. **What does the illustration show?**
   Ⓐ oceans on Earth
   Ⓑ the stars in the night sky
   Ⓒ the shape of our moon
   Ⓓ the planets around our sun

2. **What do the labels tell you?**
   Ⓐ the size of each planet
   Ⓑ the color of each planet
   Ⓒ the name of each planet
   Ⓓ how far apart the planets are

3. **The planet _____ is the largest.**
   Ⓐ Mercury
   Ⓑ Jupiter
   Ⓒ Saturn
   Ⓓ Neptune

4. **Which planet is smaller than Earth?**
   Ⓐ Uranus
   Ⓑ Mercury
   Ⓒ Saturn
   Ⓓ Neptune

STRATEGY PRACTICE Why are the planets shown in this order?

_____

_____

READ THE INFORMATION · Think about what hamster owners need to know.

Hamster Care

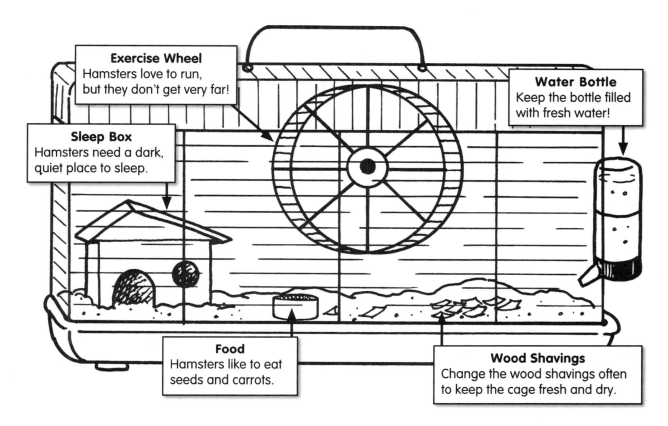

Exercise Wheel
Hamsters love to run, but they don't get very far!

Water Bottle
Keep the bottle filled with fresh water!

Sleep Box
Hamsters need a dark, quiet place to sleep.

Food
Hamsters like to eat seeds and carrots.

Wood Shavings
Change the wood shavings often to keep the cage fresh and dry.

SKILL PRACTICE · Read the question. Fill in the bubble next to the correct answer.

1. The bold words in the selection tell _____.
   Ⓐ what a hamster's cage needs
   Ⓑ where to buy hamsters
   Ⓒ why hamsters are good pets
   Ⓓ what hamsters eat

2. Why are the arrows needed?
   Ⓐ to add a design to the drawing
   Ⓑ to tell people where to learn more
   Ⓒ to show what the words tell about
   Ⓓ to show the order to look at things

3. What do the pictures help you see?
   Ⓐ how a hamster runs in a wheel
   Ⓑ how much water to put in the bottle
   Ⓒ what hamsters eat
   Ⓓ how you might set up the cage

4. What goes into the little dish?
   Ⓐ fruit
   Ⓑ seeds
   Ⓒ cheese
   Ⓓ crackers

STRATEGY PRACTICE · Show a partner the two items in the drawing that you think are the most important for a pet hamster.

Answer Key

DAY 1
Answers will vary, but students should refer to actions from the story or themes of caring about animals.
1. B   2. D   3. D   4. C

DAY 2
Answers will vary, but students should tell about a time they felt excited.
1. D   2. C   3. B   4. A

DAY 3
Answers will vary.
1. D   2. C   3. B   4. B

DAY 4
Answers will vary—e.g., "The Tortoise and the Hare."
1. C   2. B   3. A   4. C

DAY 5
Answers will vary but should be related to the theme of the story—e.g., "A time when it was hard to learn something new was when I learned to subtract."
1. C   2. D   3. A   4. B

WEEK 2

DAY 1
Answers will vary.
1. A   2. B   3. D   4. C

DAY 2
Answers will vary but should reference vivid language from the passage.
1. C   2. D   3. A   4. B

DAY 3
Answers should be vivid language from the passage—e.g., dark, thin, small, blue, green, silver, etc.
1. D   2. C   3. A   4. B

DAY 4
Answers should reference details from the passage.
1. C   2. A   3. B   4. D

DAY 5
Drawings should show details from the passage.
1. D   2. C   3. B   4. A

WEEK 3

DAY 1
things to eat
1. B   2. B   3. A   4. D

DAY 2
the third paragraph
1. B   2. A   3. B   4. B

DAY 3
how a seed grows into a plant
1. A   2. D   3. B   4. C

DAY 4
the fourth or last paragraph
1. A   2. C   3. B   4. D

DAY 5
It tells what happens first, next, and last.
1. A   2. D   3. A   4. B

WEEK 4

DAY 1
Answers will vary. Students should be able to defend their answers.
1. C   2. A   3. D   4. B

DAY 2
Students should underline steps 2, 4, 6, 8, and 9.
1. D   2. B   3. A   4. C

DAY 3
Wording will vary—e.g., "find where information is in a book"
1. B   2. D   3. C   4. A

DAY 4
First paragraph: "A row of tall trees along a city road needed to be cut down." Second paragraph: "Tucked into a hole in the tree were five baby barn owls!" Third paragraph: "They did not cut down the tree that had the baby owls in it."
1. D   2. B   3. C   4. A

DAY 5
"favorite pets in second grade"
1. A   2. D   3. C   4. B

WEEK 5

DAY 1
Questions will vary.
1. C   2. C   3. B   4. D

DAY 2
Questions will vary
1. C   2. C   3. D   4. A

DAY 3
Questions will vary.
1. A   2. C   3. D   4. B

DAY 4
Questions will vary but should reference a detail or theme from the story.
1. B   2. D   3. A   4. C

DAY 5
Questions will vary—e.g., "How did Momotaro's mother find him?"
1. C   2. B   3. B   4. D

WEEK 6

DAY 1
Students should recall three details from the passage.
1. A   2. A   3. C   4. B

DAY 2
Answers will vary—e.g., "I do agree with Jamie's mother because practice is important."
1. A   2. D   3. C   4. B

DAY 3
Answers will vary.
1. B   2. C   3. D   4. A

DAY 4
"round and brown; little hairs on the outside; hollow on the inside; white like snow."
1. D   2. B   3. A   4. A

DAY 5
Answers will vary but should include details from the passage.
1. D   2. B   3. A   4. C

WEEK 7

DAY 1
1. B   2. D   3. C   4. A
Red stands for bravery and strength, white stands for doing what is right and for saying the truth, and blue stands for fairness and hard work. The stripes stand for the first 13 states, and each star stands for a current state.

DAY 2
1. A   2. D   3. C   4. B
Answers will vary but should be main ideas.

DAY 3
1. D   2. A   3. B   4. D
Wording will vary—e.g., "string a pole," "bait a hook," "cast the line," "wait for a bite," and "turn the reel"

DAY 4
1. C   2. D   3. A   4. B
Answers will vary.

DAY 5
1. B   2. D   3. C   4. A
Answers will vary.

WEEK 8

DAY 1
1. A   2. B   3. D   4. C
Answers will vary but should indicate vivid language from the passage.

DAY 2
1. C   2. D   3. C   4. A
"makes muscles stronger; bones get stronger; helps your brain grow"

DAY 3
1. A   2. C   3. D   4. B
Answers will vary but should include descriptive adjectives and vivid verbs.

Daily Reading Comprehension • EMC 3452 • © Evan-Moor Corp.

DAY 4
1. B 2. D 3. A 4. C

First paragraph: "A baseball game is a lot of fun." Second paragraph: "The pitcher is the most interesting player to watch." Third paragraph: "It's exciting when a batter hits a home run." Fourth paragraph: "The game gets boring if nobody hits the ball." Or "Time passes slowly" Or "But get a tasty hot dog, and you'll be glad you came."

DAY 5
1. D 2. A 3. B 4. D

Students should underline details in the fourth paragraph.

WEEK 9

DAY 1
1. B 2. A 3. D 4. C

Questions will vary.

DAY 2
1. C 2. B 3. A 4. B

Answers will vary but should pick up a comparison or contrast from the passage.

DAY 3
1. B 2. C 3. D 4. A

Questions will vary but should pick up on ideas or themes in the passage—e.g., "How is a guide dog different from a pet dog?"

DAY 4
1. C 2. D 3. B 4. A

Answers will vary but should be details from the passage.

DAY 5
1. B 2. C 3. D 4. A

Questions should be answerable with information from the passage.

WEEK 10

DAY 1
1. D 2. D 3. B 4. A

Answers will vary.

DAY 2
1. B 2. A 3. D 4. C

Answers will vary but should include vivid language.

DAY 3
1. A 2. C 3. B 4. C

Responses will vary.

DAY 4
1. C 2. B 3. B 4. D

Answers will vary but should include vivid language.

DAY 5
1. B 2. D 3. A 4. C

Answers will vary.

WEEK 11

DAY 1
1. C 2. A 3. D 4. B

Answers will vary, but students should give a reason for their choice.

DAY 2
1. B 2. D 3. A 4. C

Answers will vary but should relate to details in the passage.

DAY 3
1. A 2. C 3. D 4. B

Questions will vary but should make sense in the context of the passage.

DAY 4
1. A 2. A 3. B 4. B

Answers will vary but should show a thematic or topical connection to the passage.

DAY 5
1. A 2. D 3. B 4. C

Questions will vary.

WEEK 12

DAY 1
1. B 2. A 3. C 4. D

Wording will vary—e.g., A glossary helps you learn what words mean. You use it when you find a word in a book that you don't understand.

DAY 2
1. A 2. B 3. C 4. A

Wording will vary—e.g., The table of contents tells you on what page a chapter begins.

DAY 3
1. D 2. C 3. B 4. D

when the sale happens and where it happens

DAY 4
1. B 2. D 3. C 4. C

Wording will vary—e.g., A circle graph lets you compare parts to each other or to the whole.

DAY 5
1. A 2. D 3. C 4. C

Answers will vary—e.g., The pictures and the text work together to help you understand the rules.

WEEK 13

DAY 1
1. A 2. B 3. D 4. C

Questions will vary but should be answerable with information from the passage.

DAY 2
1. B 2. B 3. D 4. C

Answers will vary.

DAY 3
1. A 2. D 3. A 4. C

Wording will vary—e.g., A tadpole looks like a black or brown ball. It learns to swim and grows teeth. Its body gets longer and grows legs. As it grows, the tail gets shorter and the face looks like a frog.

DAY 4
1. D 2. B 3. D 4. C

First, Next, Then

DAY 5
1. C 2. B 3. D 4. A

Wording will vary—e.g., Water vapor gets cold and becomes water again. Millions of water drops make clouds. When there is more water than the clouds can hold, the water falls to Earth.

WEEK 14

DAY 1
1. A 2. D 3. C 4. B

"The doctors and nurses smiled." "The sick people smiled, too." "The men and women who lived there smiled and waved from their rooms."

DAY 2
1. D 2. A 3. B 4. A

Students should underline what Kobe's father says in the second paragraph and what Kobe's brother says in the fourth paragraph.

DAY 3
1. B 2. A 3. C 4. C

Answers will vary but should include descriptive details from the passage.

DAY 4
1. B 2. C 3. B 4. A

The first two paragraphs should be circled. The third paragraph should be boxed.

DAY 5
1. D 2. C 3. D 4. A

Answers will vary but should include vivid language.

WEEK 15

DAY 1
1. A 2. C 3. B 4. D

Questions will vary.

DAY 2
1. B 2. C 3. D 4. A

Wording will vary but should include details about the cats from the passage.

DAY 3
1. C 2. A 3. B 4. D

Questions will vary but should be answerable with information from the passage.

DAY 4
1. D   2. B   3. C   4. A

Wording will vary—e.g., They planted lettuce, peas, beans, and broccoli. They listened to the First Lady talk about healthy food and eating well.

DAY 5
1. A   2. B   3. C   4. B

Questions will vary but should be answerable using information from the passage.

WEEK 16

DAY 1
1. D   2. A   3. D   4. B

Responses will vary but should show a thematic connection to the passage.

DAY 2
1. C   2. D   3. B   4. B

Wording will vary but responses should include details from the passage.

DAY 3
1. B   2. C   3. D   4. A

Answers will vary.

DAY 4
1. C   2. D   3. C   4. A

Responses will vary but should include details from the passage.

DAY 5
1. B   2. C   3. D   4. A

Answers will vary.

WEEK 17

DAY 1
1. D   2. B   3. C   4. A

Questions will vary but should be answerable with information from the passage.

DAY 2
1. B   2. A   3. C   4. D

Answers will vary.

DAY 3
1. A   2. B   3. A   4. B

Questions will vary.

DAY 4
1. C   2. B   3. D   4. A

Responses will vary.

DAY 5
1. D   2. B   3. A   4. C

Responses will vary but should not repeat information from the passage.

WEEK 18

DAY 1
1. D   2. C   3. A   4. B

Students should underline information under the headings "Monster Math" and "Fall Spelling Tree."

DAY 2
1. A   2. B   3. C   4. D

Wording will vary—e.g., The headings explain what the text below them is about.

DAY 3
1. A   2. C   3. D   4. B

Students should circle three of the following: where the classes are, when the classes are held, how much the classes cost, the phone number to call for more information.

DAY 4
1. A   2. C   3. B   4. D

Wording will vary—e.g., The menu helps you know what will be served for lunch each day of the week.

DAY 5
1. C   2. C   3. D   4. B

Wording will vary—e.g., The pictures of actors are included so that you will know the characters when you see them.

WEEK 19

DAY 1
1. B   2. D   3. A   4. C

Answers will vary but should include reasoning based on text from the passage.

DAY 2
1. C   2. D   3. B   4. A

Students should paraphrase the second sentence of the first paragraph and the first sentences of the second and third paragraphs.

DAY 3
1. A   2. B   3. C   4. D

Wording will vary—e.g., "Maria helps her aunt cook dinner. Then Maria takes a bath." Students may also infer, "Maria also goes to the lake."

DAY 4
1. C   2. A   3. B   4. D

Answers will vary, but students should be able to defend their answers.

DAY 5
1. B   2. C   3. D   4. A

Answers will vary but should refer to a main idea of the passage.

WEEK 20

DAY 1
1. B   2. D   3. C   4. A

Responses will vary but should include vivid language.

DAY 2
1. D   2. B   3. C   4. A

Students should star the second paragraph.

DAY 3
1. A   2. C   3. B   4. D

Students should recall details from the first paragraph.

DAY 4
1. C   2. D   3. A   4. B

The students played a game with a beach ball and a game of tag.

DAY 5
1. C   2. A   3. D   4. B

Wording will vary but should include vivid language from the passage.

WEEK 21

DAY 1
1. B   2. D   3. C   4. A

Responses will vary.

DAY 2
1. B   2. A   3. C   4. D

Students should reference details from paragraphs 2 and 3.

DAY 3
1. C   2. D   3. B   4. C

Questions will vary.

DAY 4
1. A   2. D   3. B   4. C

Three of the following: carrots, butternut squash—orange; flowers or raspberries—red; walnuts, tree bark—tan; strawberries—pink; grapes—purple; plant leaves—green

DAY 5
1. B   2. A   3. C   4. D

Questions will vary.

WEEK 22

DAY 1
1. B   2. C   3. D   4. A

Answers will vary.

DAY 2
1. C   2. B   3. D   4. A

Answers will vary but should reference details from the passage.

DAY 3
1. B   2. D   3. A   4. C

Responses will vary.

DAY 4
1. C   2. A   3. B   4. D

"She dropped the bat to the ground with a thump and dragged her feet as she walked to the bench."

DAY 5
1. A   2. B   3. C   4. D

Answers will vary.

WEEK 23

DAY 1
1. C   2. A   3. B   4. D

Questions will vary.